THE
INTERNATIONAL
CONSULTANT

THE INTERNATIONAL CONSULTANT

H. PETER GUTTMANN

Vice President, Stanley Consultants, Inc.
General Chairman, International Engineering and Construction Industries Council of the United States

McGRAW-HILL BOOK COMPANY

New York St. Louis San Francisco Auckland Bogotá
Düsseldorf Johannesburg London Madrid Mexico
Montreal New Delhi Panama Paris São Paulo
Singapore Sydney Tokyo Toronto

Library of Congress Cataloging in Publication Data

Guttmann, Hans Peter, date.
The international consultant.

Bibliography: p.
Includes index.
1. Consulting engineers. 2. Engineering—Contracts and specifications. I. Title.
TA157.G9 658'.91'62 76-27364
ISBN 0-07-025306-4

1234567890 KPKP 785432109876

The editors for this book were Jeremy Robinson and Betty Gatewood, the designer was Elliot Epstein, and the production supervisor was Frank Bellantoni. It was set in Baskerville by Bi-Comp.

It was printed and bound by The Kingsport Press.

To C. Maxwell Stanley

CONTENTS

FOREWORD

Never before have so many consultants from the United States been so busy competing around the world. And never have they had so much international competition.

The volume of construction work on large projects requiring professional engineering and architectural services is tremendous. And because it is concentrated in so many developing countries, which lack their own technical expertise, a very large market exists for the professional services available from private consultants in the more developed countries. From the United States, Canada, Europe, Japan, and other developed nations they go out to engineer the infrastructure of developing lands from Afghanistan to Zaire. In this age of oil in which the world now finds itself, petrodollars are generators of great new construction projects; the oil-producing countries are booming ahead.

In 1975, almost half of the 500 largest design firms in the U.S. (architects, engineers, and those who design and construct) went abroad to look for work. Forty percent actually were doing work internationally. And more than half of those working abroad were working in the oil-rich Middle East. As foreign billings for U.S. consultants hit a record high, there were 103 firms in the Mideast in 1975 on 179 active assignments valued at over $180 million in billings for professional services.

It is not only in the Middle East that large projects draw the interest and talents of international consultants. U.S. firms found 120 assignments in Africa in 1975, and 189 in Central and South America. In those areas, too, the demand for engineering and architectural services was growing.

It is not oil money alone that generates construction and the need for A/E services. International bank financing of projects stimulates international competition for professional engagements. Foreign aid programs take the donor nation's consultants abroad to work on aided projects.

Neither do international consultants do business solely in developing parts of the world. In this high-technology age, expertise is swapped about among highly industrialized countries as well. For example, U.S. consultants were at work last year in Belgium, Canada, Finland, France, Italy, Japan, West Germany, and the USSR.

Consultants from the United States were working for the Russians in the 1930s—on hydroelectric and irrigation projects. Consultants from the U.S., the U.K., and certainly all those European countries that colonized and developed parts of the world, have been sending engineering expertise abroad for many decades.

But never as now. Never has the need been greater for the consultants able to work abroad; never has the need been greater for the information that Peter Guttmann sets forth in this book.

While there is lots of work out there, it is difficult work to get, difficult work to do. Foreign markets for professional services have different dimensions, different risks. Working abroad intrigues the uninitiated. And many who venture forth fail.

Stanley Consultants, the firm Peter Guttmann serves as vice president, has enjoyed many years of working abroad, and the firm freely has shared its experience abroad through the years. It was Max Stanley who chaired the First Institute for International Engineering at the University of Colorado in Boulder in January, 1963.

It is Peter Guttmann who currently chairs the International Engineering and Construction Industries Council of the U.S. He has led in efforts through the years to increase the export of professional services from the U.S. and to improve the competitive positions of American consultants abroad.

Arthur J. Fox
President, American Society of Civil Engineers

PREFACE

International consultants are increasingly important to our world. They play an indispensable role in the pursuit of peaceful coexistence between the powerful industrialized nations and the lesser developed countries whose economy has traditionally been based on agriculture and the export of raw materials. Consultants provide advice and guidance, perform professional services where assistance is needed, supervise developments, and teach and train. They are a vital link in the transfer of technology, which is no longer an academic term but has become a fact of life.

Consultants, under the terms of this book, may be architects, economists, educators, engineers, managers, or planners. Some may work as individuals, some may work as part of small teams in highly specialized areas of professional expertise, and others could be members of firms numbering hundreds of employees with practically unlimited capabilities to execute diversified engagements for governments and private enterprise.

Consulting is not included as yet in the regular curriculum of colleges and universities. I hope very much that this void can be filled in the future. I am preoccupied by the fact that in a country as advanced as the United States of America, the function of a consultant is frequently not understood. Frankly, I am at a loss to explain how an established domestic consultant contributes at times to the confusion about his profession by an apparent ignorance of some of his duties, responsibilities, and ethics. I must admit, however, that in the international arena little has been taught to date and much has to be learned about preparing international consultants for worldwide services.

At this time, when exporters of goods and services are more interested than ever in working abroad, I have been encouraged by friends and associates to write a comprehensive handbook for the international consultant. Thus, this book is concerned with the basic approaches of a consultant to the international marketplace. I do depart from the premise that members of the various professions preparing to perform international services are fully familiar with domestic practices and eminently experienced as consultants in their chosen fields of technical expertise.

Likewise, I assume that individuals and firms proposing to serve international clients are fully aware of the need to maintain the highest ethical standards of professional conduct. During the past few years, there has been an apparent loosening of morals, a decline in honesty, and a loss of integrity in the private enterprise system as well as in governments. Serious accusations of questionable practices have been made against a number of international corporations. Professional recognition can only be achieved by professional performance. Hence, there is no room whatsoever for payoffs and kickbacks in the consulting field at home or abroad. An established consultant-client relationship can be strengthened by voluntary gestures of special cooperation and the provision of reasonable accommodations enhancing the best interest of a particular undertaking. International consultants must be prepared to exercise the greatest self-discipline and restraint in their dealings abroad.

I have given much thought to writing a chapter about the position of international consultants vis-à-vis economic boycotts, but decided against the inclusion of this controversial political subject in an essentially technical handbook.

Some readers may be disappointed because of the absence of draft contract forms, which could indeed be useful. However, there are too many alternatives that require special attention. While many clients today are using standard forms of one kind or another, contract language essentially is a matter to be handled by experienced legal counsel.

Another temptation was to attempt to explain why, since many foreign governments support their consultants, the U.S. government is remiss in providing incentives to independent American consultants in private international practice. Again, I limited my observations to the bare facts, leaving economic-commercial recomendations and conclusions to the qualified experts in this particular field.

In the following chapters, I have drawn heavily on a lifetime of international experience in diplomacy, industry, and the consulting profession. Throughout the book, I have treated consultants as masculine as a linguistic convenience and because of my personal experience in the past. There is no reason whatever to assume that women are disqualified from the performance of international services. Quite to the contrary. Along with many associates and clients I am looking forward to active participation of professionally qualified women in overseas work. Hence, wherever I have referred to "he" and "him," let it be interpreted as applying just as well to "she" and "her." It is my hope that this book will prove to be a useful aid to consultants throughout the world.

This book is dedicated to C. Maxwell Stanley, Chairman of the Board of Directors of Stanley Consultants, Inc., of Muscatine, Iowa. His vision and enterprise propelled a small consulting firm to national prominence and international recognition. I owe much of my knowledge and enthusiasm to this remarkable man, who stands tall among his peers.

C. R. (Whity) Odden, P.E. deserves special mention for his provocative advice and assistance in preparing the manuscript.

Among others who contributed, special thanks are due Robert H. Anderson, my associate and friend, Hans-Peter, Jr., my son, and Margherita, my wife, for their patience and understanding.

H. Peter Guttmann

THE WORLD'S MARKETS AND OVERSEAS COMPETITION

The marketplace for international consultants is the world—some 140 sovereign countries and territories ranging from a population of approximately 800 million to less than 500 thousand. There are many ways to look at prospective areas of interest for international operations. Markets can be classified as industrial nations or developing countries; higher-, middle-, and lower-income countries; petroleum exporters; centrally planned economies; geographical classifications; religious groupings; language blocks; etc. Fortunately, some information is readily available for any researcher, and some of it is free of charge, such as the World Bank's *Atlas,* which also contains excellent data on population, per capita gross national products (GNPs), and growth rates. This document is revised every two years.

Economists and statesmen are comfortable in the use of catch-all phrases such as "North-South relationships," "East-West Trade," "Third World Nations." While the implications need to be considered for a global marketing strategy, international consultants basically should depart from the principle of supply and demand: "We have something to offer those who can use our services!"

Naturally, countries of limited industrial development with natural and human resources employ and, in many cases, attract industrial know-how; emerging nations short of investment finance and managerial talent look for an infusion of development capital and organizational skills. However, despite the logic that the "have nots" would automatically be the perfect market for the "haves," actual conditions are not that simple at all. The main reasons are politics and economics.

For instance, from a political standpoint the free enterprise system of the United States and some of her allies is philosophically in conflict with and commercially contrary to a number of rigidly state-controlled regimes. Competitive capitalist procedures are totally opposed to socialist concepts. Also educational and procedural processes in certain countries have forged such great differences that a common ground for mutual cooperation and benefit with others is hard to find. Economically, the lack of an existing infrastructure, unfavorable balances of trade and payments, and heavy existing debt servicing may effectively impede otherwise perfectly natural relationships. The world's markets, therefore, need to be carefully analyzed from many different angles on an individual basis.

Consulting is a service. Consultant practices are a service industry, and international consulting is an export of services. While the matters of expertise, experience, and availability are normally the prime considerations to any exporter of services, the acceptance of the consultant's nationality, policies, and procedures, and the facilities of the prospective client or the importer are frequently a very close second. For example, the Republic of Guatemala will presently not permit the employment of British consultants because of a controversy over Belize. Citizens of Belgium are once again very popular in the Republic of Zaire where, for a few years, they were certainly less than welcome; the Dutch went through a similar period in Indonesia. Also, there are instances where the regulations of some governments will not allow their own consultants to serve in certain other countries, such as United States citizens in Cuba, Taiwanese in the People's Republic of China, Albanians in Yugoslavia, etc.

Traditional relationships and common interests undergo constant changes. In international political and economic affairs, what might have been regarded as a sound alliance yesterday may be subject to critical review today and considered objectionable tomorrow. The ease of worldwide communications and short intercontinental travel time contribute to shifts of policy. Also, an emphasis from imports to exports and vice versa can completely alter long-established alignments and trade patterns. It must therefore be concluded that (1) world markets need continuous attention by all who want to serve them; (2) new appraisals are in order following even apparently minor local, regional, national, and international developments; and (3) gradual changes should be anticipated just as unexpected ones will occur from time to time.

WORLD STATISTICS

The World Bank Group, in its 1975 *Annual Report,* divides the emerging nations into six geographical groupings: East Africa; Western Africa; East Asia and the Pacific; South Asia; Europe, the Middle East, and North Africa; and Latin America and the Caribbean. The following is a summary of the authoritative, relevant statistics that should be of interest.

EAST AFRICA	POPULATION (000)*	PER CAPITA GNP (US$)
Botswana	641	240
Burundi	3,580	70
Ethiopia	26,550	90
Kenya	12,480	180
Lesotho	1,165	120
Malagasy Republic	7,610	140
Malawi	4,833	110
Mauritius	860	350
Rwanda	3,980	70
Somalia	3,042	90
Sudan	17,051	130
Swaziland	459	300
Tanzania	13,974	120
Uganda	10,829	140
Zaire	23,438	90
Zambia	4,646	390

* Estimated as of mid-1973.

East Africa

The 16 countries in East Africa are heavily dependent on the export of a small number of primary products to earn the foreign exchange required to pay for imports.

During 1975, Ethiopia, Kenya, Somalia, and Tanzania suffered severe setbacks from continuing drought, and Mauritius was hit by one of the worst cyclones in its history. Political changes in Ethiopia and the Malagasy Republic affected the ability of these two nations to deal with economic problems. Zaire and Zambia found themselves badly hurt by the drop in copper prices whereas only a few years ago the rising price of the metal had sharply increased their revenues. Burundi, Ethiopia, Kenya, the Malagasy Republic, and Rwanda also were disappointed because of lower coffee prices, which had peaked in 1974. Hence, Eastern Africa as a whole registers very slow progress with only one exception—Botswana, where the start-up of exploitations of diamond, copper, and nickel resources provided a substantial boost in its earning capacity.

Development activities in East Africa include education and manpower training, raising of agricultural productivity, investment in land development, transport, mining, and housing.

WESTERN AFRICA	**POPULATION** (000)*	**PER CAPITA GNP** (US$)
Cameroon	6,206	220
Central African Republic	1,710	170
Chad	3,870	70
Congo	1,199	310
Dahomey	2,947	110
Equatorial Guinea	306	250
Gabon	520	960
The Gambia	493	120
Ghana	9,313	300
Guinea	5,243	100
Ivory Coast	5,600	360
Liberia	1,452	330
Mali	5,370	70
Mauritania	1,257	190
Niger	4,304	90
Nigeria	71,262	170
Senegal	4,070	270
Sierra Leone	2,787	190
Togo	2,105	170
Upper Volta	5,714	70

* Estimated as of mid-1973.

Western Africa

Conditions in Western Africa were greatly influenced recently by domestic political developments and abrupt changes in commodity and other prices. While the Sahelian countries started the slow road to recovery from the effects of the drought, the early effects of declining activity and demand from industrialized nations is being felt.

Specifically Nigeria, but also Gabon and the People's Republic of the Congo benefited from exports of petroleum; Gambia, Nigeria, and Senegal improved profitable exports of groundnuts; Senegal and Togo did well in phosphates; and Guinea earned foreign exchange with bauxite shipments. Cameroon, Ghana, and the Ivory Coast, depending on cocoa, coffee, and timber sales, did not do as well. Development activities in general were subject to downward adjustments because of rising levels of expensive energy consumption and the higher cost of capital goods associated with industrialization.

Immediate and future concerns of Western Africa are food and livestock production, education, telecommunications, and transportation.

EAST ASIA AND THE PACIFIC	POPULATION (000)*	PER CAPITA GNP (US$)
Cambodia	7,566	110
Republic of China	15,424	570
Fiji	551	570
Indonesia	124,415	100
Korea, Republic of	32,910	370
Laos	3,180	70
Malaysia	11,750	480
Papua New Guinea	2,596	340
Philippines	40,123	270
Singapore	2,185	1,580
Thailand	39,400	240
Socialist Republic of Vietnam **	40,000	110
Western Samoa	153	200

* Estimated as of mid-1973.
** As of June 1976.

East Asia and the Pacific

For much of the East Asia and Pacific region, the decline in world market prices of major export commodities, notably rubber, timber, and coconut products, means lesser income. High import prices for fuel, foodstuffs, and capital equipment has worsened many terms of trade. Korea has been particularly affected; even Indonesia, despite increased oil revenues, continues in financial straits; and the Philippines is experiencing a reversal of trade balances from surplus to deficit.

Food is a major factor in the area, with a number of countries attempting to achieve self-sufficiency in grain production. Thailand, however, is benefiting from high prices for its rice exports. Korea, formerly a food-surplus country, is now a net importer and working hard to be back in balance in the early 1980s. All countries except Singapore are predominantly agricultural, but industry is becoming increasingly important to growth and development. Korea and Singapore, with considerable manufacturing capabilities, are now exporting to Japan and the United States. The Philippines and Malaysia also show industrial promise by vying for further growth in their export markets.

Well endowed with human and natural resources, the East Asia and Pacific region as a whole receives large inflows of external capital. However, the Philippines, Malaysia, and Indonesia face new, inflationary problems. While high oil prices help Malaysia's balance of trade, Korea, the Philippines, and Thailand are seriously strained.

Development activities are concerned with industrial growth: infrastructure, public utilities, agricultural research, public health and education, and, in a number of countries, the systematic progress of urban and rural areas.

SOUTH ASIA	POPULATION (000)*	PER CAPITA GNP (US$)
Bangladesh	74,000	70
Burma	29,509	90
India	581,911	120
Nepal	12,020	90
Pakistan	66,230	150
Sri Lanka	13,180	110

* Estimated as of mid-1973.

South Asia

The 800 million people of South Asia are among the poorest in the world. With rising import prices for foods and declining exports, Bangladesh, Sri Lanka, India, and Pakistan are generally facing deteriorating terms of trade. Because of the extreme poverty in the region, all but Nepal are currently on the list of the UN's emergency roster of countries "most seriously affected" by recent world economic developments. Sizable amounts of money and credits are flowing into the area from the International Monetary Fund (IMF), the World Bank, the Organization of Petroleum Exporting Countries (OPEC), and others. Nevertheless, progress is very slow and, in fact, is once again seriously threatened by poor harvests. Population growth still is ahead of food production.

Bangladesh's import prices have risen during 1974 by about 94 percent as against higher export prices of less than 30 percent. Pakistan, beset by floods in August 1973 and then by a drought during most of 1974, suffered great agricultural setbacks. In addition, Pakistan experienced costly delays in the completion of the Tarbela Dam. Only Burma, because of high prices for its rice, had some reason for optimism. However, the need for imports places a heavy burden on its economy. Nepal, always in need of petroleum, cement, and fertilizer, had a negative balance of payments; Sri Lanka, though increasing exports of tea, rubber, and coconut, fell badly behind in its balance of payments in 1974. India's plight, of course, is common knowledge.

EUROPE, THE MIDDLE EAST, AND NORTH AFRICA	POPULATION (000)*	PER CAPITA GNP (US$)
Afghanistan	15,219	90
Algeria	14,700	460
Bahrain	232	670
Cyprus	655	1,290
Egypt	35,619	250
Finland	4,660	3,170
Greece	8,970	1,670
Iran	32,136	570
Ireland	3,030	1,760
Israel	3,210	2,790
Jordan	2,540	290

EUROPE, THE MIDDLE EAST, AND NORTH AFRICA (*continued*)	POPULATION (000)*	PER CAPITA GNP (US$)
Lebanon	2,970	900
Morocco	16,200	290
Oman	618	620
Portugal	8,560	1,130
Romania	20,830	890
Spain	34,740	1,360
Syria	6,942	370
Tunisia	5,459	410
Turkey	37,930	400
Yemen Arab Republic	6,217	100
People's Democratic Republic of Yemen	1,560	110
Yugoslavia	20,960	890

* Estimated as of mid-1973.

Europe, the Middle East, and North Africa

Developments in this region in fiscal 1975 were strongly influenced by the increase in the price of oil, worldwide inflation and its impact on import prices, the deterioration in the terms of trade of developing countries, and the recession in the industrialized nations.

Only Afghanistan, the Yemen Arab Republic, and the People's Republic of Yemen have annual per capita incomes of less than US$200 and depend so heavily on imports of food, fertilizers, manufactured goods, and petroleum that they, as well as Egypt, qualify for the UN's list of "most seriously affected" countries, requiring special international emergency assistance. Eight major petroleum exporters—Algeria, Iran, Iraq, Kuwait, Libya, Qatar, Saudi Arabia, and the United Arab Emirates—fall in the categories of middle and higher per capita income of developing countries, accumulating a surplus of some US$53 billion in 1974.

Greece, Portugal, Spain, Turkey, and Yugoslavia are facing some deterioration in their economies because of increases in the price of oil and capital goods and lesser income from tourism and workers' remittances. However, Morocco and Tunisia are doing well mainly because of exports of phosphates.

LATIN AMERICA AND THE CARIBBEAN	POPULATION (000)*	PER CAPITA GNP (US$)
Argentina	24,282	1,410
Bolivia	5,331	230
Brazil	101,051	720
Chile	10,230	760
Colombia	23,777	440
Costa Rica	1,872	710
Dominican Republic	4,432	530
Ecuador	6,727	390
El Salvador	3,801	370
Guatemala	5,175	520
Guyana	772	400
Haiti	4,454	120
Honduras	2,781	330
Jamaica	1,967	860
Mexico	56,047	810
Nicaragua	1,973	520
Panama	1,570	940
Paraguay	2,416	350
Peru	14,531	590
Trinidad and Tobago	1,059	990
Uruguay	2,995	780
Venezuela	11,279	1,260

* Estimated as of mid-1973.

Latin America and the Caribbean

The recent trends in the international economy have had significant but divergent effects on Latin America and the Caribbean. Almost everywhere, higher import prices and lower export prices created unexpected problems.

Petroleum exporters—Bolivia, Ecuador, Trinidad and Tobago, and particularly Venezuela—did well in 1974; Argentina, Colombia, and Mexico are almost self-sufficient in petroleum, but Brazil, Chile, Jamaica, and Uruguay depend entirely on oil imports, and therefore suffered severe economic reverses. Barbados, the Dominican Republic, and Guatemala benefited from higher world prices for sugar; while the exports of bauxite generated income increases for the Dominican Republic, Haiti, and Jamaica. Lower copper prices depressed Chile and Peru; Argentina, Paraguay, and Uruguay had reduced export earnings from wool.

The recession in the industrial countries was felt in some of the nations that have achieved some economic diversification: Argentina, Brazil, Colombia, and Mexico, as demand declined for manufactured goods; and tourism is falling off in the Bahamas, Barbados, Haiti, Jamaica, and Mexico.

A U.S. CONSULTING A/E'S REVIEW

From the point of view of a U.S. consultant in architecture, economics, engineering, management, and planning, the greatest international market potential currently lies with the petroleum-exporting nations. These are the countries whose exports generate substantial income for development and where ambitious plans are being pursued for accelerated programs such as the world has never seen before. Obviously, the technology, industrial performance, managerial know-how, and development experience of the United States have enabled its consultants to help less fortunate people around the globe to improve their lot. If statistics and forecasts are to be believed, the petroleum-exporting nations, particularly those of the Middle East and North Africa, can be expected to represent a multibillion dollar market for international consultants over the next ten years. Services required include the establishment of whole new cities with transportation systems, provision of utilities, construction of health and educational facilities, highly sophisticated industrial complexes, communication centers, and assistance in agricultural developments.

The oil-producing countries have long been beneficiaries of consulting services and as such are no strangers to international practices and procedures governing the service industry. Nevertheless, conditions are now being imposed on international consultants that are neither traditional nor customary, and are often difficult to meet. Hence, while the Middle East market is certainly by far the most active and lively as this is being written, it also presents substantial difficulties in many respects. I am afraid that quite a few consultants may find it impossible to fulfill some of the obligations that they accepted in the enthusiasm of "hot pursuit" of a first engagement in a new, promising market. It will have to be seen how much of a shake-out this will cause the consulting profession during the next few years.

Proceeding to some of the other world markets, once again from the point of view of the generalist consulting organization operating from the United States, East Asia and the Pacific will continue to provide challenges and work. In many areas there, Americans are still regarded as liberators; politically, therefore, the United States is favorably positioned. Economically, however, the region is not within the traditional American area of influence. And several countries are accustomed to working on a friendly basis with some of their former colonial masters and the more industrialized and developed nations in the area.

Latin America and the Caribbean, as opposed to East Asia and the Pacific, has historically been regarded as an area of United States interest and concern. Indeed, throughout the Central and South American republics and the Caribbean states, there exist close economic and commercial ties with the United States that provide for a natural consulting relationship. To many international consultants based in North America, the countries south of the Rio Grande have been valued clients and good friends. There is no reason to anticipate that this will not continue for many years into the future despite occasional political flare-ups. However, it must be recognized that much of Latin America, particularly from an educational standpoint, can no longer be regarded as underdeveloped. Many of the leading professionals there have been educated in universities and centers of higher learning in Europe and the United States and are accumulating practical working experience that amply qualifies them to perform the professional work that has up to now been performed by foreign consultants in their countries. Yet it is reasonable to predict that Latin America and the Caribbean Islands will continue to constitute an active market for consultants from the United States for many years to come. However, the services to be performed will be increasingly limited to areas of high technology and management, and foreign firms will find that their engagements will require associations, joint venturing, and other forms of close cooperation with host-country individuals and firms.

The continent of Africa represents a marketing area and a potential that is rarely understood by Americans. The sheer size of Africa often overpowers otherwise experienced international executives who have not been personally involved in that part of the world. Since the last colonial ties have been severed only recently, considerable shifts in attitudes and relationships can be anticipated for the future. Africa is rich in natural resources and has a large and growing population to support. While there exist political differences between the various African states, and also among tribes and regions within a single state, the continent as a whole presents one of the world's greatest opportunities for development—a situation that should continue well into the middle of the next century. Infrastructure will have to be planned; local, national, and international communications need to be set up; natural resources developed; and agriculture, industry, and commerce established to satisfy the demands of the Africans themselves and the needs of the rest of the world.

Europe is, with few exceptions, a highly industrialized continent long accustomed to offering consulting services around the world. Technical know-how, combined with the traditional drive to export, has established the Scandinavians, Germans, British, French, and Italians as our greatest competitors. Nevertheless, for an interdependent world, high technology combined with economic and financial interests and historic ties sometimes provides a common base for joint efforts. Thus, our consultants are applying advanced American technology in Europe and both European and American consultants are frequently pooling their talents and working together in the emerging nations.

India, Pakistan, and Bangladesh are countries that have provided enormous challenges to consultants for several decades. Projects that have been undertaken and accomplished on the Indian subcontinent in the twentieth century under the direction of international consultants could well have been included in the wonders of the world of only a few hundred years ago. Unfortunately, the enormous domestic needs of these three nations to feed and educate their steeply increasing populations exceed all available resources. The present reluctance to commit vast amounts of money for the kind of development work that employs international consultants makes it somewhat doubtful that the American services industry will find expanding marketing possibilities in that area of the world in the near future.

POLITICAL AND ECONOMIC VIEWS

East-West trade has been much in the news lately, along with détente, disarmament, the Strategic Arms Limitation Talks (SALT), and other international negotiations and treaties. Whereas only a few years ago there existed practically no relationship between the United States and the Union of Soviet Socialist Republics, today many hundreds of millions of dollars flow from the East to the West, and much of this is in payment for the export of technology. Independent consultants in private practice will not find it easy to offer and perform their services in the Socialist republics, simply because competitive capitalist practices are alien to state-directed enterprises. Currently, very few consultants have found the opportunity to attract the attention of the Socialist republics. The demand has been mainly for professionals who, in combination with constructors, owners of processes for oil refineries, chemical plants, steel mills, and other industrial facilities, can propose and furnish whole plants from design through completion, preferably including financing. Still, the needs of the East are so great that it is not impossible to anticipate that differences in philosophy and politics can and will be overcome. Personally, I am convinced that in years to come the U.S.S.R. and the Socialist republics of the East represent the greatest potential of all future markets for American consultants.

Similar to some extent, and yet very different, is the situation with the People's Republic of China. A country with an enormous population, a proud tradition, and thousands of years of independence and sometimes isolated national development, China today is fundamentally different from much of the rest of the world. One of the intriguing aspects of China's status quo is its contention that its development in the future must be entirely different from that of the rest of the world. Hence, there exist currently very few areas of common interest where international consultants would be welcome to contribute to China's development. The situation is not very much different from the one that existed, say, twenty-five years ago, between the U.S.S.R. and many countries in the West. Hence, changes may occur in the next decade or so. Because of China's enormous wealth and population, it is a country to be watched closely as a potential marketplace for American consultants.

Finally, in reviewing the world markets, one cannot overlook the single most important trade partner of the United States, namely Canada. While our neighbor to the north imports more from the United States than any other country, consulting services in Canada are mainly furnished by Canadians and/or other nationals who have settled in Canada proper. Canada, as a matter of fact, competes strongly with the services exported by other industrialized nations. However, Canada itself is a strongly developing and industrializing nation and requires professional assistance from time to time, mainly because it simply does not have the trained personnel to go it alone. Unfortunately, tariff barriers and customs restrictions do not make it easy for U.S. consultants to work up north. Yet ways and means have been found in the past and will be found in the future for continued cooperation; hence Canada has to be included as a potential marketplace for U.S. consultants.

As an additional guide to the international marketplace, the U.S. Department of Commerce, basing its listing upon current imports of American goods and services, annual anticipated growth rate of imports, and American industry's opinion, has targeted the following countries as special areas of marketing interest for the United States:

1. Japan
2. United Kingdom
3. Germany
4. France
5. Brazil
6. Mexico
7. Scandinavia
8. Arab Countries
9. Singapore and Malaysia
10. Australia and New Zealand
11. Venezuela
12. Italy
13. Iran
14. Taiwan
15. Netherlands
16. Spain and Portugal
17. Central America
18. Belgium and Luxembourg
19. Israel
20. Korea
21. Indonesia
22. Switzerland
23. Hong Kong
24. Caribbean
25. Philippines
26. Yugoslavia
27. Nigeria
28. Colombia
29. Algeria
30. Zaire
31. Argentina

A review of the world's markets would not be complete without an individual look at two nations in the Western Hemisphere and a few others that are outstanding because of their importance and environment. Mexico, our southern neighbor, is a country that is quickly developing into one of the major Latin American industrial economies. Following North American practices and procedures, Mexico is attuned to the use of consultants but furnishes most of these from its own nationals. However, those Mexican industries with connections in the United States frequently call upon this country for expertise and advice; large public-works-type and government-sponsored undertakings may be well served by joint consulting activities. Therefore, the Mexican market potential, while limited to some extent, certainly is present and should not be ignored. Brazil is another nation that commands attention because of its potential. Rich in natural and human resources and dynamic in its development, Brazil stands out among the Latin American nations as a country with a great future. Set apart from the rest of the continent because of the Portuguese language, the Brazilians work closely and successfully with consultants from all over the world. Brazil is definitely one of the major consulting markets of the present and for the future.

Nigeria, in West Africa, is a country that has been identified as a "comer" ever since it achieved independence from Great Britain in

1960. With more than 70 million people and a strong favorable trade balance derived from exports of petroleum, Nigeria is the prototype of the developing nation that is straining all its resources to do the most in the least possible time. The consulting involvement in Nigeria is extremely heavy at this time, and will continue to grow in the future. Quite a few observers agree that Nigeria is one of the top seven international marketplaces for American consultants, the others being Kuwait, the United Arab Emirates, Saudi Arabia, Iran, Algeria, and Brazil.

COMPETITION

It is quite obvious, of course, that any searching investigation of the world's markets must include an examination of the competition that can be expected to be found. There is an ancient proverb that says "Fish where the fish are." Clearly, consultants from all over the world converge upon those areas where projects within their competence are expected to develop and where it is reasonable to assume that international consultants will be engaged. In years past, a number of relatively simple conclusions had been drawn concerning market preferences and coverage:

1. Colonies, trust territories, and small countries in the shadow of large developed nations give preference to consultants of their rulers, protectors, and important neighbors.
2. Newly independent and relatively inexperienced nations count on the continued support of their former rulers and frequently prefer to continue to look for consulting support from the same sources.
3. Sovereign and fully independent states, new and old, select their advisers from among the most advanced and progressive consultants they can find.

A review of recent history indicates drastic changes from these concepts. Political, economic, and, to some extent, local and regional considerations are increasingly becoming of greater importance in the selection of consultants than past cooperation and a spotless record of good professional performance and achievement. Thus, there is no hard and fast rule as to who competes against whom and where. Every major project represents a case that has to be individually examined. If an undertaking is to be financed by one of the international financial institutions and development agencies, it is only reasonable to assume that the selection of consultants for the work to be performed will be limited to member-country nationals of these organizations. As long as there exist political differences and international friction, consultants of friendly countries will be selected in preference to those from strictly neutral or opposing nations. If financing is a major consideration, consultants who have known connections and can obtain economic assistance will be preferred. Thus, only after these and a good many other possible considerations will a prospective client look at the consultants' expertise, experience, and availability, which in the professionals' criteria should really be of the first order of importance.

Additionally, many countries nowadays do wish to see their nationals involved in consulting work and demand some kind of participation, ranging from the simple registration of a foreign firm to a majority position in joint ventures. Even the best qualified foreign consultant will not be able to expect selection if he is not prepared or able to satisfy such basic local requirements, despite the fact that nationalism and restrictive local practices in the last few years are known to have contributed to a number of serious setbacks to large and important international undertakings.

International Competitors

Who are the most active consultants in the international marketplace in addition to North Americans? First of all, the Europeans, composed of groups of Scandinavians, Dutch, Germans, British, French, Italians, Spanish, Swiss, Portuguese (almost exclusively directed toward their former colonies and Brazil), and Belgians (working mostly in French-speaking countries and Zaire in particular). Canadians have considerable exposure worldwide; Australians and New Zealanders are working more widely in Asia. Israelis offer their services wherever they are politically acceptable; the Japanese are most aggressive and persistent in their quest to excel in the exports of services and goods.

In Latin America, Colombia has developed international consulting experience and skills that permit her firms to work not only locally but also throughout the southern part of the hemisphere and into other continents; Brazilians and lately Mexicans have started programs to assist some of their neighbors by providing financing and direct support for their firms. Chile, Costa Rica, and Uruguay have long been known to provide highly educated and well-trained consultants who not only offer the expertise from their homeland but also actually emigrate with their families and settle in the countries where their services are in demand.

U.S. consultants in private practice generally adhere to a code of ethics that is regarded as basic and inviolable. Essentially, a North American professional strives to achieve standards of excellence in the performance of his professional services, to serve his clients in an unbiased and capable manner, and to warrant their goodwill and confidence while earning a fair fee. The same kind of professionalism is not always observed by all international competitors. French firms, for instance, are frequently controlled by the French government and, therefore, cannot be expected to perform as truly independent consultants. German industries and banks use consultants as salesmen to promote their interests, offering at times free consulting services in return for imported goods, particularly equipment orders. The Japanese more often than not are a branch of large, powerful trading companies whose final objective is to participate in upcoming projects through every one of the elements of construction, delivery of capital goods, etc.

To complicate matters further, many countries actually set up consortia to compete as one unit on specific international prospects, thereby eliminating internal competition from among their own nationals and uniting against international competition. U.S. consultants, of course, are limited in any kind of consortium approach that could lead to the selection of determined market areas by preselected groups because of domestic antitrust legislation that is applicable on foreign work. This pitches the North Americans not only against each other but in addition against superbly well-organized international teams.

Governments Support Their Nationals

In the international marketplace it is no longer unusual to find foreign consultants working hand in hand with foreign governments. As I mentioned above, France, for example, having a proprietary interest in a large number of consultants and industries, openly steps into carefully determined markets to promote French firms. The United Kingdom has been known to support British consultants all the way from introductions through recommendations, and if that is not enough, by applying diplomatic pressure for the award. Spain finances grants, from time to time, under the condition that Spanish firms, exclusively, be selected for the execution of the works. Israel provides financing to developing countries with the stipulation that only Israeli nationals become engaged and then appoints these directly with the single criterion of benefiting as much as possible politically and/or materially thereby.

It is interesting to note that governments have started to comprehend the importance of having their nationals engaged as international consultants overseas. A clear understanding has been reached in many countries that if one of their nationals becomes involved in the early stages of a large international project, fellow countrymen will have the best opportunities to benefit from the follow-up activities, such as the delivery of goods, equipment, and services. In realizing this fact, more and more governments have quietly injected themselves to strengthen their international consultants and to make their nationals more competitive in the international marketplace. In addition to using official sources to gather commercial and technical intelligence, chambers of commerce, government-to-government missions, commercial and economic attachés, and sometimes even ranking members of the foreign service can be found promoting new business activities. And as if this were not enough, indirect sales tools have been developed and are being used, such as export incentives, tax rebates, performance guarantees, full insurance at low premium cost, etc. Since the cost of consulting services is important to the client and frequently becomes a decisive factor in the final selection and award of a contract, government support can considerably influence a firm's overhead and net income after taxes. Governments, therefore, have become major competitive elements in the international marketplace.

The United States, following a tradition of "hands off" and free enterprise, has been conservative and quite reluctant to follow the protectionist attitudes of other governments. In a recent study of the assistance that governments provide to their exporters, it was revealed that of eight major categories, United States exporters of goods and services are only partially supported in one. (See the table on p. 19.)

The support of various governments has, of course, greatly influenced the competitiveness of international consultants, and can contribute substantially toward the final selection and award process. Despite the fact that it can stifle independent judgment of a consultant's professional capability, expertise, and experience, government interference is now a factor in the international marketplace that cannot be ignored and that must be taken into consideration.

Official government assistance to promote exports is not limited to the service industry. Information published in late November 1975 by the U.S. Department of Commerce indicates that in 1974, the official

	USA	FRANCE	GER-MANY	UK	JAPAN	ITALY
Insurance against currency fluctuation	no	yes	yes	yes	yes	yes
Tax rebate on exports	no	yes	yes	yes	no	yes
Indirect tax incentives for exports	no	yes	yes	yes	no	yes
Tax exemptions	no	yes	no	yes	yes	yes
Protection against export losses	no	yes	yes	yes	yes	no
Direct export tax incentives	no	yes	no	yes	yes	no
Partial or total exemption of foreign branch income	no	yes	yes	no	no	no
Deferral of export income	yes	yes	yes	no	yes	no
Summary of eight export incentives	1	8	6	6	5	4

agencies of the Common Market and Japan supported about $56 billion in exports of goods and services as against $12.5 billion made available in the United States by the Export-Import Bank, in direct credits. Further, during 1974, the Common Market expanded a number of programs to protect their members from production cost increases; the British introduced a new inflation risk insurance plan that could absorb an estimated $130 million for the first year. Even more generous is a reported inflation cover program by the French, for which $225 million has been earmarked for the first year.

CONCLUSION

The world's markets and overseas competition represent opportunities and challenges of absolutely enormous proportions. Powerful governments, international financiers, nationals from many countries, and some of the world's most renowned professionals compete against each other. There exist only few rules that are acknowledged by all—the stakes are high, as the engagements signify prestige and profits. A seasoned consultant remarked recently at an international workshop: "There is more work in the international marketplace than all the established consultants in the world could handle during the next twenty-five years. But only a fraction of all that work is going to be commissioned, and it will go to but a fraction of the profession who are the most aggressive, the best prepared, and the ones with the strongest support."

For the convenience of the reader, the following is a listing of the sovereign nations of the world with information about their capital cities, official languages, and dates of independence. This should be of assistance for elementary universal market research and appraisal.

COUNTRY	PRIMARY LANGUAGE(S)	CAPITAL	YEAR OF INDEPENDENCE
Afghanistan	Pushtu, Dari	Kabul	1921
Albania	Albanian	Tirana	1918
Algeria	Arabic, French	Algiers	1962
Angola	Portuguese	Luanda	1975
Argentina	Spanish	Buenos Aires	1816
Australia	English	Canberra	1901
Austria	German	Vienna	
Bahamas	English	Nassau	1973
Bahrain	Arabic	Manama	1971
Bangladesh	Bengali, English	Dacca	1971
Barbados	English	Bridgetown	1966
Belgium	French, Flemish	Brussels	1839
Bhutan	Bhutanese	Thimbu	1971
Bolivia	Spanish	La Paz, Sucre	1825
Botswana	English, seTswana	Gaborone	1966
Brazil	Portuguese	Brasília	1822
Bulgaria	Bulgarian	Sofia	1878
Burma	Burmese	Rangoon	1948
Burundi	French	Mujumbura	1962
Cambodia	Khmer	Phnom Penh	1955
Cameroon	French, English	Yaoundé	1960/61
Canada	English	Ottawa	1867

COUNTRY	PRIMARY LANGUAGE(S)	CAPITAL	YEAR OF INDEPENDENCE
Central African Republic	French	Bangui	1960
Chad	French	Njamena	1960
Chile	Spanish	Santiago	1818
China, People's Republic of	Chinese (Mandarin)	Peking	
China, Republic of	Chinese (Mandarin)	Taipei	1946
Colombia	Spanish	Bogotá	1819
Congo, People's Republic of the	French	Brazzaville	1960
Costa Rica	Spanish	San José	1821
Cuba	Spanish	Havana	1902
Cyprus	Greek, Turkish	Nicosia	1960
Czechoslovakia	Czech, Slovak	Prague	1918
Dahomey	French	Porto Novo	1960
Denmark	Danish	Copenhagen	
Dominican Republic	Spanish	Santo Domingo	1844
Ecuador	Spanish	Quito	1830
Egypt	Arabic	Cairo	1952
El Salvador	Spanish	San Salvador	1821
Equatorial Guinea	Spanish	Malabo	1968
Ethiopia	Amharic, English	Addis Ababa	
Fiji	English	Suva	1970
Finland	Finnish	Helsinki	1917
France	French	Paris	
Gabon	French	Libreville	1960
Gambia	English	Banjul	1965
German Democratic Republic	German	East Berlin	1945
German Federal Republic	German	Bonn (Berlin)	1945
Ghana	English	Accra	1957
Great Britain	English	London	
Greece	Greek	Athens	1830
Grenada	English	St. George's	1974
Guatemala	Spanish	Guatemala City	1821
Guinea	French	Conakry	1958
Guinea-Bissau	Portuguese	Bissau	1974

COUNTRY	PRIMARY LANGUAGE(S)	CAPITAL	YEAR OF INDEPENDENCE
Guyana	English	Georgetown	1966
Haiti	French	Port-au-Prince	1804
Honduras	Spanish	Tegucigalpa	1821
Hungary	Hungarian	Budapest	1918
Iceland	Icelandic, English	Reykjavik	
India	Hindi, English	New Delhi	1947
Indonesia	Bahasa Indonesia	Djakarta	1949
Iran	Persian (Farsi)	Tehran	
Iraq	Arabic, Kurdish	Baghdad	1932
Ireland	Irish, English	Dublin	1921
Israel	Hebrew, Arabic	Jerusalem (Tel-Aviv)	1948
Italy	Italian	Rome	1861
Ivory Coast	French	Abidjan	1960
Jamaica	English	Kingston	1962
Japan	Japanese	Tokyo	
Jordan	Arabic	Amman	1946
Kenya	KiSwahili, English	Nairobi	1963
Korea, People's Democratic Republic of	Korean	Pyongyang	1948
Korea, Republic of	Korean	Seoul	1948
Kuwait	Arabic	Kuwait	1961
Laos	Lao	Vientiane	1954
Lebanon	Arabic	Beirut	1941
Lesotho	English, Sesotho	Maseru	1966
Liberia	English	Monrovia	1847
Libyan Arab Republic	Arabic	Tripoli	1951
Luxembourg	French	Luxembourg	1839
Malagasy Republic	Malagasy, French	Tananarive	1960
Malawi	English, Chichewa	Lilongwe	1964
Malaysia	Malay, English	Kuala Lumpur	1963
Maldives	Dihevi	Malé	1965
Mali	French	Bamako	1960
Malta	English	Malta	1964
Mauritania	French	Nouakchott	1960
Mauritius	English	Port Louis	1968

COUNTRY	PRIMARY LANGUAGE(S)	CAPITAL	YEAR OF INDEPENDENCE
Mexico	Spanish	Mexico City	1821
Mongolia	Mongolian	Ulan Bator	
Morocco	Arabic	Rabat	1956
Mozambique	Portuguese	Laurenco Marques	1975
Namibia	Afrikaans	Windhoek	(UN Trust)
Nepal	Nepali	Katmandu	1923
Netherlands	Dutch	The Hague	1814
New Zealand	English	Wellington	1907
Nicaragua	Spanish	Managua	1821
Niger	French	Niamey	1960
Nigeria	English	Lagos	1960
Norway	Norwegian	Oslo	1905
Oman	Arabic	Masqat	1971
Pakistan	Urdu, English	Islamabad	1947
Panama	Spanish	Panama City	1903
Papua New Guinea	English	Port Moresby	1974
Paraguay	Spanish	Asunción	1811
Peru	Spanish	Lima	1821
Philippines	Filipino, English, Spanish	Quezon City (Manila)	1946
Poland	Polish	Warsaw	
Portugal	Portuguese	Lisbon	1910
Qatar	Arabic	Doha	1971
Rhodesia	English	Salisbury	1965
Romania	Romanian	Bucharest	1878
Rwanda	French, Kinyarwanda	Kigali	1962
Saudi Arabia	Arabic	Riyadh	1902
Senegal	French	Dakar	1960
Sierra Leone	English	Freetown	1961
Singapore	Chinese (Mandarin), Malay, Tamil, English	Singapore	1960
Somali Republic	Arabic, Italian, French	Mogadishu	1960
South Africa	English, Afrikaans	Pretoria, Capetown	1961

COUNTRY	PRIMARY LANGUAGE(S)	CAPITAL	YEAR OF INDEPENDENCE
Spain	Spanish	Madrid	
Sri Lanka	Sinhala	Colombo	1948
Sudan	Arabic	Khartoum	1956
Surinam	Dutch	Paramaribo	1975
Swaziland	SiSwati, English	Mbabane	1968
Sweden	Swedish	Stockholm	
Switzerland	German, French, Italian	Bern	
Syrian Arab Republic	Arabic	Damascus	1946
Tanzania	Swahili, English	Dar-es-Salaam	1961
Thailand	Thai	Bangkok	
Togo	French	Loné	1960
Trinidad and Tobago	English	Port-of-Spain	1962
Tunisia	Arabic, French	Tunis	1956
Turkey	Turkish	Ankara	1923
Uganda	English, KiSwahili	Kampala	1962
U.S.A.	English	Washington, D.C.	1776
U.S.S.R.	Russian	Moscow	
United Arab Emirates	Arabic	Abu-Dhabi	1971
Upper Volta	French	Ouagadougou	1960
Uruguay	Spanish	Montevideo	1825
Venezuela	Spanish	Caracas	1830
Vietnam, Socialist Republic of	Vietnamese, French	Hanoi	1975
Yemen Arab Republic	Arabic	Sana	1962
Yemen, People's Democratic Republic of	Arabic	Aden	1967
Yugoslavia	Serbo, Croat	Belgrade	1918
Zaire	French	Kinshasha	1960
Zambia	English	Lusaka	1964

HOW TO SPOT AND ZERO IN ON FOREIGN PROSPECTS

The question most frequently asked by consultants interested in overseas work is: "How can I find out where a job is coming up?" Unfortunately, there is no simple answer to this question. However, a great many sources of professional, industrial, institutional, and commercial data are available. Some come completely free of charge, others at surprisingly low cost, and a few at such a high cost that they have yet to prove their worth in order to justify the expense.

Any effective consulting organization in pursuit of "new business" must be well informed both technically and procedurally in administration and professional matters. After all, a consultant's raison d'être is to provide guidance, know-how, and leadership. Individuals and firms can neither enter the international marketplace nor survive there unless they are fully up to date on past and current domestic and international developments, important political affairs, and economic factors.

BE INFORMED

A primary source of day-by-day happenings is the morning edition of a national (not local) newspaper. This can be complemented with one or two weekly magazines covering domestic and international events. In addition, professional literature reporting on technical matters and overseas marketing should be consulted. It is not excessively difficult to develop a generalized and fairly accurate appreciation of current local, national, and overseas developments.

My own reading list includes *The New York Times, The Washington Post,* and *The Wall Street Journal,* daily; *The Journal of Commerce, Time,* and *Business Week,* weekly; plus some technical and professional publications that come across my desk with articles of particular interest. I spend an average of an hour and a half per day just reading. Much of my understanding of the world in which we live and work has always come from these readily available sources.

SOURCES OF INFORMATION

Within the professional community, an increasing number of associations and societies encourage their members to be international in their scope of knowledge. Even experienced overseas executives admit that they benefit from occasional exchanges of information with their peers. Also, beginners in a foreign practice may do well to use their professional contacts as an opportunity to express their desire to become involved. Those who are established abroad usually find it useful to have a roster of available local consultants on whom they can draw for support in such areas as specialized, high-technology expertise; extended production facilities; personnel; financial support; etc. The first rule for an international practice is to be known, the second is to be respected, and the final is to be recognized.

Much industrial work, including the transfer of technology, is undertaken by the large multinational (transnational) corporations. More often than not, these industries are quite willing to take their domestic consultants with them into foreign lands, particularly when these employees are already familiar with company policies, practices, and specific needs.

However, to facilitate assimilation and create goodwill in their new locations, many multinational corporations also seek to employ local expertise and enlist cooperation from the nationals of the host countries. A hitherto domestically oriented individual or firm should therefore seriously entertain the option of joining forces with others, either by a contractor-subcontractor relationship or through associations and joint ventures. This would include not only the staff of the primary industrial client but also nationals of foreign countries. The subject of associations and joint ventures with host-country individuals and firms is covered in Chapter 8 of this book.

Commercially, a whole new "service industry" has developed during the past decade, selling information by means of conferences, workshops, newsletters, market analyses, etc. Some of these are very much worth the input of time and expense; others will be found too generalized, after-the-fact, and unreliable. As no consultant can expect to be successful without efficient, comprehensive, and accurate commercial intelligence, it may take special effort to select only those services that will be useful.

In addition to the media and industrial-commercial sources, a number of the international development institutions and financing agencies can provide valuable information about forthcoming as well as ongoing projects. Such information may be used by the general public.

Consultants should be on record with every one of the international organizations that finance, and at times commission, service contracts within the professional's area of interest. A few agencies will automatically place serious international consultants on their mailing lists upon receipt of registration forms. Chapter 9, "The International Development Institutions and Financing Agencies," provides considerable information in this connection.

Registration of a consultant's expertise, experience, and fields of endeavor is both important and necessary, not only in order to be included on mailing lists for annual reports, sector papers, speeches, statistics, and news releases, but also to receive occasional invitations to submit proposals directly, or to be approved as acceptable, if selected by a borrower.

Filing complete registration statements with the numerous international agencies is a time-consuming and cumbersome process. Several national professional societies and international federations are currently making efforts to standarize the official forms and punch-cards that are being used by the various organizations. Unfortunately, little progress has been reported to date. Troublesome as it may be, there is no alternative for the consultant but to prepare and submit the required documentation to each and every of the many agencies.

General brochures, perfectly acceptable in the industrialized countries, are often dubbed "picture books" by skeptical international contract officers and are frequently discarded. At best, a standard brochure may be regarded as complementary to the official documentation and registration package. Therefore, instructions as to how a firm or an individual should list details covering expertise, past history, staffing, working experience over a period of usually five years, foreign language speaking capabilities, etc., must be followed with the very greatest of care and as much in depth as possible.

Within the United States, much useful information can be obtained from the Office of International Marketing, Bureau of International

Commerce, U.S. Department of Commerce; officials of the Agency for International Development (AID); the Export-Import Bank of the United States (EX-IM); the Overseas Private Investment Corporation (OPIC); the Foreign Credit Insurance Association (FCIA); and desk officers of the U.S. Departments of State and Commerce, all with offices in Washington, D.C. The International Reading Room, in the Department of Commerce building in Washington, contains an excellent library, able personnel, and the necessary facilities to research the international marketplace and to obtain copies of documents from the government, agencies, institutions, and development banks at a very nominal fee. The U.S. Department of Commerce, incidentally, maintains district offices in forty-three cities throughout the continental United States, Puerto Rico, Hawaii, and Alaska, and will service inquiries about foreign trade.

A number of foreign chambers of commerce and associations generate information and can provide introductions to interested consultants. Here is a current list of these:

FOREIGN CHAMBERS OF COMMERCE AND ASSOCIATIONS IN THE UNITED STATES

Africa

African-American Chamber of Commerce, Inc.
99 Church Street
New York, New York 10007

Arabia

American-Arab Association for Commerce and Industry, Inc.
505 Fifth Avenue
New York, New York 10017

American-Arab Chamber of Commerce
319 World Trade Building
Houston, Texas 77002

U.S.-Arab Chamber of Commerce
1 World Trade Center
Suite 2645
New York, New York 10048

Argentina

Argentine-American Chamber of Commerce
11 Broadway
New York, New York 10004

Austria

U.S.-Austrian Chamber of Commerce, Inc.
165 West 46th Street
New York, New York 10036

Belgium

Belgian-American Chamber of Commerce in the U.S., Inc.
50 Rockefeller Plaza
Suite 1003-1005
New York, New York 10020

Brazil

Brazilian-American Chamber of Commerce, Inc.
22 West 48th Street
New York, New York 10036

Chile

Chile-American Association, Inc.
220 East 81st Street
New York, New York 10028

The Chamber of Commerce, Industries and Tourism of Chile and California
79 Central Avenue
San Francisco, California 94117

China

Chinese Chamber of Commerce of New York
180 Park Row
New York, New York 10038

Chinese Chamber of Commerce of San Francisco
730 Sacramento
San Francisco, California 94108

Colombia

Colombian-American Chamber of Commerce, Inc.
55 Liberty Street
New York, New York 10005

Dominican Republic

Dominican Chamber of Commerce of the United States, Inc.
1270 Sixth Avenue
New York, New York 10009

Ecuador

Ecuadorean-American Association, Inc.
55 Liberty Street, Room 804
New York, New York 10005

Far East

Far East–America Council of Commerce and Industry
1270 Avenue of the Americas
New York, New York 10020

Finland

The Finnish-American Chamber of Commerce
540 Madison Avenue
New York, New York 10022

The Finnish-American Chamber of Commerce of the Midwest
1 IBM Plaza
Chicago, Illinois 60611

The Finnish-American Chamber of Commerce on the Pacific Coast
3600 Wilshire Boulevard
Los Angeles, California 90005

France

French Chamber of Commerce in the United States, Inc.
1350 Avenue of the Americas
New York, New York 10019

Germany

German-American Chamber of Commerce of the Pacific Coast, Inc.
465 California Street
San Francisco, California 94104

German-American Chamber of Commerce of Chicago
77 East Monroe Street
Chicago, Illinois 60603

German-American Chamber of Commerce, Inc.
666 Fifth Avenue
New York, New York 10019

Greece

Hellenic-American Chamber of Commerce
25 Broadway
New York, New York 10004

India

India Chamber of Commerce of America, Inc.
501 Fifth Avenue, Suite 1809
New York, New York 10017

India-American Commerce Association of Chicago
3434 North Halsted Street
Chicago, Illinois 60657

Indonesia

American-Indonesian Chamber of Commerce, Inc.
120 Wall Street
New York, New York 10005

Iran

Iranian-American Chamber of Commerce
Overhill Building
Scarsdale, New York 10583

Ireland

Ireland–United States Council of Commerce and Industry, Inc.
460 Park Avenue
New York, New York 10022

Israel

American-Israel Chamber of Commerce and Industry, Inc.
11 East 44th Street
New York, New York 10017

American-Israel Chamber of Commerce and Industry, Inc., Midwest Chapter
180 North Michigan Avenue
Chicago, Illinois 60601

American-Israel Chamber of Commerce and Industry
Cleveland Chapter
500 One Public Square Building
Cleveland, Ohio 44113

American-Israel Chamber of Commerce and Industry
Detroit Chapter
Suite 210, 19900 West Nine Mile Road
Southfield, Michigan

American-Israel Chamber of Commerce and Industry
Philadelphia Chapter
211 South Broad Street
Philadelphia, Pennsylvania 19107

California-Israel Chamber of Commerce in Los Angeles
P.O. Box 36042
Los Angeles, California 90036

Italy

Italian Chamber of Commerce of Chicago
327 South LaSalle Street
Chicago, Illinois 60604

Italy-America Chamber of Commerce, Inc.
350 Fifth Avenue, Suite 3015
New York, New York 10001

Italian-American Chamber of Commerce of the Pacific Coast
World Trade Center, Room 258
San Francisco, California 94111

Japan

Japanese Chamber of Commerce of New York, Inc.
39 Broadway
New York, New York 10006

Japanese Chamber of Commerce of Chicago
232 North Michigan Avenue
Chicago, Illinois 60601

Japanese Chamber of Commerce of Northern California
World Trade Center, Room 137
San Francisco, California 94111

Korea

Korean-American Midwest Association of Commerce and Industry
c/o Northwest Orient Airlines, Inc.
29 East Madison Street
Chicago, Illinois

Korea-American Commerce and Industry Association
Suite 2-L
88 Morningside Drive
New York, New York 10027

Latin America

Central American Chamber of Commerce, Inc.
99 Church Street
New York, New York 10007

Chamber of Commerce of Latin America in the United States, Inc.
One World Trade Center, Suite 3549
New York, New York 10048

Lebanon

United States–Lebanese Chamber of Commerce, Inc.
5 World Trade Center
New York, New York 10048

Malaysia

Malaysian-American Chamber of Commerce
P.O. Box 2801
Washington, D.C. 20013

Mexico

Mexican Chamber of Commerce of Los Angeles
125 East Sunset Boulevard
Los Angeles, California 90012

The Mexican Chamber of Commerce of the United States, Inc.
5 World Trade Center, Suite 6343
New York, New York 10048

United States–Mexico Chamber of Commerce
1800 K Street, N.W., Suite 410
Washington, D.C. 20006

The Netherlands

The Netherlands Chamber of Commerce in the United States, Inc.
1 Rockefeller Plaza
New York, New York 10020

Netherlands Chamber of Commerce in the United States (For the Pacific Coast States), Inc.
Los Angeles World Trade Center
333 South Flower Street, Suite 901
Los Angeles, California 90071

The Netherlands Chamber of Commerce in the United States, Inc.
Wrigley Building, Suite 638
410 North Michigan Avenue
Chicago, Illinois 60611

Nigeria

Nigerian-American Chamber of Commerce, Inc.
99 Church Street
New York, New York 10007

Norway

The Norwegian-American Chamber of Commerce
1300 South Beacon Street
San Pedro, California 90731

Norwegian-American Chamber of Commerce
244 California Street
San Francisco, California 94111

Norwegian-American Chamber of Commerce, Inc.
360 North Michigan Avenue
Chicago, Illinois 60601

Norwegian-American Chamber of Commerce, Inc.
800 Foshay Tower
Minneapolis, Minnesota 55402

The Norwegian-American Chamber of Commerce, Inc.
800 Third Avenue
New York, New York 10022

Pakistan

Pakistani-American Chamber of Commerce, Inc.
501 Fifth Avenue, Suite 1809
New York, New York 10017

Peru

Peruvian-American Association
11 Broadway
New York, New York 10004

The Philippines

The Philippine-American Chamber of Commerce, Inc.
565 Fifth Avenue, Room 903
New York, New York 10017

Philippine Chamber of Commerce of America, Inc.
24 California Street
San Francisco, California 94111

Spain

Spain–United States Chamber of Commerce, Inc.
500 Fifth Avenue
New York, New York 10036

Spain–United States Chamber of Commerce of the Middle West
55 East Washington Street
Chicago, Illinois 60602

Spain–United States Chamber of Commerce of the Pacific Coast, Inc.
Room 668, 612 South Flower Street
Los Angeles, California 90017

Sweden

Swedish-American Chamber of Commerce, Inc.
1 Dag Hammarskjold Plaza
New York, New York 10017

Swedish-American Chamber of Commerce of the Western United States, Inc.
World Trade Center, Ferry Bldg.
San Francisco, California 94111

Trinidad and Tobago

Trinidad and Tobago Chamber of Commerce of the United States of America, Inc.
400 Madison Avenue
New York, New York 10017

United Kingdom

British-American Chamber of Commerce
10 East 40th Street
New York, New York 10016

British-American Chamber of Commerce and Trade Center of the Pacific Southwest
530 West Sixth Street, Suite 520
Los Angeles, California 90014

British-American Chamber of Commerce and Trade Center
Suite 809, 310 Sansome Street
San Francisco, California 94104

British-American Chamber of Commerce
333 South Flower St., Suite 562
Los Angeles, California 90017

British-American Chamber of Commerce
68 Post Street, Suite 714
San Francisco, California 94104

Venezuela

Venezuelan Chamber of Commerce of the United States, Inc.
501 Fifth Avenue, Suite 1809
New York, New York 10017

Diplomats stationed in the embassies of foreign nations in Washington can be helpful from time to time, but normally are not in a position to furnish realistic information about the exact status of plans, prospects, and projects in their respective countries. This does vary from embassy to embassy. However, official country missions are usually very well informed. They may be on their way to New York for meetings with the United Nations and the United Nations Development Programme or to Washington for reviews, appraisals, and sophisticated economic discussions with the International Monetary Fund, the International Bank for Reconstruction and Development, the Interamerican Development Bank, and the Organization of American States.

I have more than once benefited very much from getting together, here in Washington, with an important and busy minister of state of a foreign nation who is normally practically inaccessible in his own country. One of my earliest engagements in Latin America came about through a personal visit with a ranking minister of economy. He had been much too busy to see me in his offices at home but was most grateful for whatever little I was able to do for him while he was delayed in Washington during protracted loan agreement negotiations with an international agency.

Attempting to zero in on a particular project may well be rewarded by obtaining current knowledge of the movements and travels of foreign dignitaries. Some ranking officials, as a matter of fact, expect their consultants to meet with them during their travels, and I have personally experienced more than once how a courtesy visit consolidated past relationships and brought about new engagements.

Clearly, spotting a foreign prospect requires considerable perserverance, much hard work, and occasionally, a bit of good luck. Then too, a sound, proven professional experience with satisfied past clients sometimes produces repeat engagements, referrals, and recommendations. More than this, however, is usually required by the intense competition of international markets. New business development overseas depends greatly upon skillful professional exposure, aggressive personal and institutional connections, and positive industry recognition.

Almost everywhere in the world where private enterprise is active, services can be offered and promoted in many diverse ways. There are the professional cards printed in publications that are circulated widely in many countries throughout the world. These are frequently read by prospective clients. For the ambitious consultant, there are always opportunities to write occasional articles for technical magazines having international distribution, or to deliver a paper and lecture at appropriate overseas meetings. Universities and professional societies are generally most grateful for voluntary participation on the part of foreigners in their programs, particularly in the less developed countries. Student councils and societies with an international membership likewise welcome outsiders. None of these efforts will guarantee contracts, but all are steps in the right direction.

NEW BUSINESS PROMOTION

Let there be no doubt, regardless of all the above preparatory steps, and others which have not been specifically mentioned, by far the largest number of overseas engagements are obtained by means of direct contacts abroad. Nothing surpasses the personal approach—to be in the right spot at the right time with all homework done and with the needed expertise and production facilities at a cost to the clients that can be considered competitive.

Without painstaking homework, the decisive tête-à-tête with a prospective client may never come about. On the other hand, if after careful preparations the consultant arrives in an active market at the appropriate time, then indeed, he has overcome one of the most daunting initial difficulties and is on the way. No longer is it a question of finding out where a job is coming up. Instead, the next step is obvious. Now comes the time to zero in, to spot specific prospects, and to identify clients.

Worldwide travel is one of the basic requirements for any international consultant. A great deal of intelligence can be gathered in the United States, and some contacts can be made locally. However, it is indispensable to follow through abroad and sometimes in more than just one place, particularly if the client and the financier happen to be located in separate areas, which occurs quite frequently. For instance, if a large sanitary-type project, say in Thailand, has come to a consultant's attention, it may be best for him to visit first with the financiers, such as the World Health Organization in Geneva and the Asian Development Bank in Manila, and only then with the Thais in Bangkok.

Altogether, it is not only advisable but absolutely essential on the highly competitive international scene to get to know as much as possible about everything even remotely connected that might have a bearing on the new undertaking. Time and again, when calling on prospective clients abroad, I have received only a lukewarm response to an initial routine introductory call. But, once my host found out that I did have some knowledge concerning his project, that I had learned of past trials and errors, that I knew some of the personalities involved (just to mention one kind of approach), I was no longer only one of the dozens of consultants who call on him every month. Instead, I was suddenly an honored guest—one of the few who had made an impression and would be remembered in the future.

It must be recognized that when the daily newspapers and weekly magazines report new development plans and activities in a distant country, a consultant has probably already performed some general advisory services and thereby may be in line as the most natural candidate for the execution thereof. This applies particularly to cases of prefeasibility and preinvestment studies. By the time news releases inform the public about loan agreements, special fund transactions, and grant concessions leading to projects financed by the international financial institutions and development agencies, consultants have normally been involved. After all, somebody had to provide the guidance and advice to the borrower who eventually brought about the very project execution of the announcement. Naturally, these same consultants, in most cases, can be expected to continue with the undertaking. However, from time to time, extended services and additional skills may be required. Thus, it can be concluded that, in order to be given the full opportunity to perform international services as a prime consultant (perhaps to be shortlisted first and then to be selected after submitting a proposal), very early direct contacts with prospective clients are absolutely essential.

I have previously mentioned the advantage of having good, solid contacts within the professional community for combined efforts with others; now let us take a look at the overseas markets, where the work originates and engagements can be expected. Many foreign governments today are well aware of the value of experienced international consultants. Thus, a number of countries have established points of contact. Professionals in search of upcoming work are invited to visit these and be briefed about proposed developments, upcoming projects, and the executive agencies. A number of such official information centers are given below.

NATIONAL CONTACT POINTS OF INTEREST TO INTERNATIONAL CONSULTANTS

Ministère des Affaires Etrangères
Division des Organisations Internationales
Section Coopération Multilatérale
Algiers, Algeria

Subsecretaría de Desarrollo
Dirección de Administración del Desarrollo
Hipolito Yrigoyen 250
6° Piso, Oficina 638
Buenos Aires, Argentina

The Director
Investigations and Consultancy Section
Trade Services Division
Department of Overseas Trade
Canberra, A.C.T. 2600, Australia

Ministry of Foreign Affairs
Abteilung 10
Ballhausplatz 2
A-1010 Vienna, Austria

Planning Section
Ministry of Development and Engineering Services
Manama, Bahrain

Office Belge du Commerce Extèrieur
Service des Organisations Internationales (Service 441)
World Trade Centre
Boulevard Emile Jacqmain, 162,
1000 Brussels, Belgium

Ministry of Finance and Development Planning
Division of Economic Affairs
Private Bag 8
Gaborone, Botswana

Ministry of Planning
Sub-Secretariat for Technical and International Co-operation
Brasília, Brazil

Ministerski Savet
Komissia Ilonomitchesko l Nautchno-Technitshesko Satrudnitchestvo
Sofia, Bulgaria

Foreign Economic Relations Department
Ministry of Planning and Office of the Ministries
Rangoon, Burma

Ministère du Plan
Phnom Penh
Cambodia

Direction de la Programmation au
Ministère du Plan et de
l'Aménagement, du Territoire
Boîte Postale 250
Yaoundé, Cameroon

Market Development Group
Department of Industry, Trade
and Commerce
112 Kent Street, Place de Ville
Ottawa KlA OH5, Canada

Ministère de l'Information
Boîte Postale Numero 373
Bangui
Central African Republic

Direction du Plan et des Aides
Extèrieures à la Présidence de la
République
Fort Lamy, Chad

Comisión Nacional Cientifica y
Technológica (CONICYT)
Avenida Canada 308
Santiago, Chile

Dirección de Organismos y
Conferencias Internacionales
(DOCI)
Ministerio de Relaciones Exteriores
de Cuba
Havana, Cuba

Ministry of Foreign Affairs
Nicosia, Cyprus

Polytechna
Technical Cooperation Agency
Panska 6
Prague 1
Czechoslovakia

Udenrigsministeriets
Handelsafdeling
Amaliegade 18
1256 Copenhagen
Denmark

Secretario Técnico de la Presidencia
(Encargado de la Coordinación
de la Asistencia Técnica Externa)
Avenida Mexico Numero 6
Santo Domingo
Dominican Republic

Development Consultants
Association (DCA)
1119 Kourneish El Nil Street
Cairo, Egypt

Imperial Ethiopian Government
Planning Commission
Addis Ababa, Ethiopia

Bundesstelle Für
Aussenhandels-Information (BFA)
5 Köln/Rhein
Blaubach 13
Federal Republic of Germany

The Secretary
Ministry of Finance
Government Building
Suva, Fiji

Export Promotion Bureau
Ministry for Foreign Affairs
Kitkansillanranta 3A
00530 Helsinki 53
Finland

Ministère des Affaires Etrangères
Bureau de Coopération
Multilatérale
36, Rue La Perouse
75775 Paris, Cedex 16
France

Principal Secretary
Economic Planning and External
Aid
P.O. Box M 76
Accra, Ghana

Consejero del Ministro
Ministerio de Economia
Palacio Nacional
Guatemala City, Guatemala

Ministry of Economic Development
High Street
Georgetown, Guyana

Chief of Section
Hungarian Chamber of Commerce
Rosenberg HP.U. 17
Budapest, V., Hungary

Idnthrounaratofnun Islands
(The Industrial Developing
Institute of Iceland)
Skipholt 37
Reykjavik, Iceland

Under-Secretary
Ministry of Finance
Department of Economic Affairs
New Delhi, India

Deputy Managing Director
Plan Organization for Technical
Affairs
Teheran, Iran

Institute for Planning and
Development (1970) Ltd.
123 Hashmonaim Street
Tel-Aviv 67011, Israel

Ministry of Foreign Affairs
Rome, Italy

Deputy Secretary
External Aid Division
Ministry of Finance and Public
Planning
P.O. Box 3007
Nairobi, Kenya

Ministry of Commerce and
Industry
Kuwait

La Commissariat Général au Plan
Ministère du Plan et de la
Coopération
Vientiane, Laos

Ministry of Foreign Affairs
Monrovia, Liberia

Ministère des Affaires Etrangères
5 Rue Nôtre Dame
Luxembourg

Ministère des Affaires Etrangères
Avenue Jean Assolant
Tananarive
Madagascar

Direction Générale de la
Coopération Internationale au
Ministère des Affaires Etrangères
Bamako, Mali

The Director of Industry
Department of Industry
30 South Street
Valletta, Malta

Ministry of Economic Planning and
Development
Port Louis, Mauritius

Dirección General de Cooperación
Técnica Internatiónal
Secretaría de Relaciones Exteriores
Avenida Nonoalco Numero 1
México, D.F. México

Department for Technical
Co-operation with UN
State Committee for External
Economic Relations
Ulan-Bator, Mongolia

Government Economic
Information Service
Department O.A.M.
Bezuidenhoutseweg 151
The Hague, Netherlands

Ministry of Foreign Affairs
Wellington, New Zealand

Commissariat Général au
Developpement
(Centre de Documentation)
Niamey, Niger

Norwegian Agency for
International Development
(NORAD)
Dronning Mauds GT. 11
Oslo, Norway

General Planning Institute
Ministry of Economy
Aden, People's Democratic
Republic of Yemen

The Chairman
National Economic Council
Manila, Philippines

The Secretary for Commerce
Private Bag
Pretoria-TVL
Republic of South Africa

Ministerul Afacerilor Externe
Directia Organizatii Internationale
Bd./Republicii NR. 33
Bucharest, Romania

Ministère de la Coopération
Internationale
B.P. 179, Kigala
Rwanda, Central Africa

Secretariat d'Etat Auprès du
Premier Ministre Chargé du Plan
Dakar, Sénégal

Ministry of Planning and
Co-ordination
Mogadiscio, Somalia, East Africa

Tecniberia
Velazquez
Madrid 6, Spain

Under-Secretary
Works Department
Ministry of Housing
P.O. Box 300
Khartoum, Sudan

International Projects
The Swedish Export Council
Storgatan 19
Box 5513
Stockholm S-114-85
Sweden

Division du Commerce
Département Fédéral de
l'Economie Publique
3000 Berne, Switzerland

State Planning Commission
Damascus, Syria

Permanent Secretary
Ministry of Planning and
Development
Trinidad House
St. Vincent Street
Port of Spain, Trinidad and
Tobago

Ministry of Industry and
Technology
(Sanayi Ve Teknoloji Bakanligi)
Mustersarlik Yazi Isleri Burosu
Ankara, Turkey

State Committee on New
Technology to the State Planning
Commission of the Ukranian SSR
12/2 Kirov Street
Kiev-8 252008
Ukranian SSR

Ministry of Foreign Affairs
Abu-Dhabi
United Arab Emirates

Export Services Division (GES 7A)
Department of Trade and Industry
Export House, 50 Ludgate Hill
London EC4M 7HU
United Kingdom

Direction du Plan et des Etudes de
Développement
Ouagadougou, Upper Volta

Export Information Reference
Room
Bureau of International Commerce
Office of Export Development
Room 1063
U.S. Department of Commerce
Washington, D.C. 20230
U.S.A.

State Committee of the Council for
Ministers of the USSR on
External Economic Relations
Moscow, U.S.S.R.

Senior Officer
Ministry of Information
Sana'a
Yemen Arab Republic

Ministry of Development, Planning
and National Guidance
P.O. Box R.W. 268
Ridgeway
Lusaka, Zambia

UNITED STATES EMBASSIES AND TRADE CENTERS

When one must start from scratch abroad, the economic and commercial officers in the American embassies overseas are good initial points of contact. Practically all our foreign missions have well-documented background information on the political, economic, and industrial developments within their jurisdiction. Files are available covering local firms, professionals, associations, agencies, and the full names and titles of important functionaries. And introductions are arranged upon request. For very special occasions, it is no longer out of the ordinary to enlist official support of the ambassador or the deputy chief of mission.

There are a number of United States Trade Centers situated in important cities around the world. A new service recently inaugurated by personnel working out of these is to provide secretarial and other assistance to the American traveler at a very reasonable cost. Every United States citizen visiting any one of the cities below can expect assistance in more than one way from these centers. They are staffed with competent, knowledgeable personnel and geared to provide reasonable support. Here is a list of current United States trade centers:

Avenue de Paris
Beirut, Lebanon
Tel. 240800

Avenida Quintana 441
Buenos Aires, Argentina
Tel. 41-8075 or 42-1110

D6000 Frankfurt-Main
Bockenheimer Landstrasse 2-4
Germany
Tel. 72-08-011

4/5 Langham Place
London W.l, England
Tel. 499-9000

Calle Liverpool
Mexico l, D.F.
Tel. 591-01-55

Via Gatta Melata 5
20149 Milan, Italy
Tel. 46-96-451

15 Chaykovskovo
Moscow, U.S.S.R.
Tel. 255-4848

123 Avenue Charles de Gaulle
92200 Neuilly, France
Tel. 624-33-13

82 Sejong Ro
Seoul, Korea 110
Tel. 72-2601/9

Yean San Building
268 Orchard Road
Singapore 9
Tel. 373-100

Vasagatan 11, S-101
Stockholm, Sweden
Tel. 24-84-20

Royal Exchange
Sydney, N.S.W. 2000
Tel. 24-6635

261 Nanking East Road
Section 3
Taipei, Taiwan
Republic of China
Tel. 782171 or 333551 ×234

61 Elizabeth Blvd.
Tehran, Iran
Tel. 623-536/7

Tameike-Tokyu Building
1-14 Akasaka 1-Chome
Minato-Ku, Tokyo 107
Tel 584-2311 ×220

Prinz Eugenstrasse 8-10
A-1040 Vienna, Austria
Tel. 65-8787

Ulica Wiejska 20
Warsaw, Poland
Tel. 21-45-15/16 or 21-63-27

While the United States of America is promoting the interests of American trade, the World Bank and the Regional Development Banks have found it expedient to maintain local offices in a number of countries to service their needs. The staffing of these outlying offices varies considerably from location to location. However, general information is usually available to the bona fide inquirer, and in some of the emerging nations, bank representatives are known to go out of their way to provide consultants with useful information and assistance. The international financial institutions and lending agencies per se are discussed in detail in Chapter 9 of this book. World Bank and Inter-American Development Bank offices are listed below:

WORLD BANK OFFICES

Headquarters: 1818 H Street, N.W., Washington, D.C. 20433, U.S.A.

New York Offices: c/o United Nations, Room 2245, Secretariat Buildings, New York, New York 10017
120 Broadway (15th Floor), New York, New York 10005, U.S.A.

European Office: World Bank, 66, avenue d'léna, 75116 Paris, France

London Office: World Bank, New Zealand House (15th Floor), Haymarket, London, SW1 Y4TE, England

Tokyo Office: World Bank, Kokusai Building, 1-1 Marunouchi 3-chome, Chiyoda-ku, Tokyo 100, Japan

Eastern Africa: World Bank Regional Mission, Extelcomes House, Haile Selassie Avenue, Nairobi, Kenya; mailing address, P.O. Box 30577

Western Africa: World Bank Regional Mission, Immeuble Shell, 64, avenue Lamblin, Abidjan, Ivory Coast; mailing address, B.P. 1850

Afghanistan: World Bank Resident Mission, P.O. Box 211, Kabul, Afghanistan

Bangladesh: World Bank Resident Mission, Bangladesh Bank Building (4th Floor), Motijheel Commercial Area, G.P.O. Box 97, Dacca, Bangladesh

Cameroon: World Bank Resident Mission, B.P. 1128, Yaoundé, Cameroon

Colombia: Resident Mission Banco Mundial, Edificio Aseguradora del Valle, Carrera 10 No. 24-55, Piso 17, Bogotá D.E., Colombia

Ethiopia: World Bank Resident Mission, I.B.T.E. New Telecommunications Building (First Floor), Churchill Road, Addis Ababa, Ethiopia; mailing address, IBRD Mission, P.O. Box 5515

Ghana: World Bank Resident Mission, c/o Royal Guardian Exchange Assurance Building, Head Office, High Street (5th Floor), Accra, Ghana; mailing address, P.O. Box M27

India: World Bank Resident Mission, 53 Lodi Estate, New Delhi 3, India; mailing address, P.O. Box 416

Indonesia: World Bank Resident Staff, Jalan Wahid Hasyim 100/102, Jakarta, Indonesia; mailing address, P.O. Box 324/JKT

Nepal: World Bank IBRD Resident Mission, R.N.A.C. Building (First Floor), Katmandu, Nepal; mailing address, P.O. Box 798

Nigeria: World Bank Resident Mission, 30 Macarthy Street, Lagos, Nigeria; mailing address, P.O. Box 127

Pakistan: World Bank Resident Mission, P.O. Box 1025, Islamabad, Pakistan

Sudan: World Bank Resident Mission, 28 Block 2H, Baladia Street, Khartoum, Sudan; mailing address, P.O. Box 2211

Tanzania: World Bank Resident Mission, N.I.C. Building (7th Floor, B), Dar es Salaam, Tanzania; mailing address, P.O. Box 2054

Thailand: World Bank Regional Mission, Udom Vidhya Building, 956 Rama IV Road, Sala Daengh, Bangkok 5, Thailand

Upper Volta: World Bank Resident Mission, B.P. 622, Ouagadougou, Upper Volta

Venezuela: World Bank Resident Mission, Centro Andres Bello, Avenida Andres Bello, 113-E, Mariperez, Caracas, Venezuela

Zaire: World Bank Resident Mission, Building UZB, avenue des Aviateurs, Kinshasa 1, Republic of Zaire; mailing address, P.O. Box 14816

Zambia: World Bank Resident Mission, P.O. Box 4410, Lusaka, Zambia

World Bank offices move frequently, as projects under way require more supervision than simple representation or routine planning. The above list is current for the year 1975, but may undergo changes in the future.

INTER-AMERICAN DEVELOPMENT BANK OFFICES

Argentina
Cerrito 264, 3er Piso
Casilla de Correo No. 181
Sucursal 1
Buenos Aires, Argentina

Barbados
Nile House, Nile Street
P.O. Box 402
Bridgetown, Barbados

Bolivia
Calle Ayacucho 277, 2do Piso
Casilla No. 5872
La Paz, Bolivia

Brazil
Rua Melvin Jones No. 5-30 Andar
Caixa Postal No. 728 ZC-00
Rio de Janeiro, Brasil

Chile
Bandera 52, 7°. Piso
Casilla No. 14315
Correo 21
Santiago, Chile

Colombia
Carrera 10a. No. 16-39 10° Piso
Apartado Aereo No. 12037
Bogotá, Colombia

Costa Rica
Calle 4 entre Avenidas
3 y 5
Apartado Postal No. 4647
San José, Costa Rica

Dominican Republic
Avenida John F. Kennedy esquina
Avenida Lopez de Vega
Edificio Nova Scotia, Cuarto Piso
Apartado Postal No. 1386
Santo Domingo, Republica
Dominicana

El Salvador
Edificio Montecristo 4° Piso
Plaza Las Americas
Apartado Postal No. (01) 199
San Salvador, El Salvador

Ecuador
San Gregorio 120
Esquina 10 de Agosto, 5°Piso
Apartado Postal 154-A
Quito, Ecuador

Europe
Banque Interamericaine de
Développement
17 Avenue Matignon
75008 Paris, France

Guatemala
Edificio ETISA, 7° Piso
Plazuela España, Zona 9
Apartado Postal No. 935
Guatemala City, Guatemala

Haiti
Rue Dantes Destouches No. 30
Boîte Postale 1321
Port-au-Prince, Haiti

Honduras
Edificio Midence Soto, 8° Piso
Apartado Postal No. C-73
Tegucigalpa, Honduras

Jamaica
2nd Floor, Imperial Life Building
Knutsford Boulevard
P.O. Box 429
Kingston 10, Jamaica

Mexico
Paseo de la Reforma 379, Piso 7
México 5, D.F., México

Nicaragua
Multicentro El Camino de Oriente
Kilometro 6 Carretera a Masaya
Apartado Postal 2512
Managua, Nicaragua

Panama
Edificio de Diego
Avenida Balboa y Calle 40
3er Piso
Apartado No. 7297
Panama 5, Panama

Paraguay
Edificio City
Estrella 345- 2do Piso
Casilla 1209
Asunción, Paraguay

Peru
Avenida Republica de Chile 388
7° Piso
Apartado Postal No. 3778
Lima, Peru

Trinidad and Tobago
80 Independence Square N.
P.O. Box 68
Port of Spain, Trinidad

Uruguay
Edificio del Banco de Credito
18 de julio 1455
Oficinas 603 y 604
Montevideo, Uruguay

Venezuela
Torre Phelps, 23° Piso
Plaza Venezuela
Apartado Postal No. 4344
Carmelitas, Caracas 101
Caracas, Venezuela

Again, as in the case with the World Bank, Inter-American Bank offices in Latin America move from time to time and while the above addresses are the current ones for 1975, changes can be expected in the years to come.

American chambers of commerce are active in many countries and do provide information and introductions. Here is a list of these:

AMERICAN CHAMBERS OF COMMERCE ABROAD

Chief Executive Officers

Argentina

J. Baldwin Robinson, General Manager
The American Chamber of Commerce in Argentina
Av. R. Saenz Pena 567
1352 Buenos Aires, Argentina
Phone: 33-5591/5592
Cable: USCHAMBCOM
Telex: 0121900

Australia

Kevin Bannon, Executive Director
The American Chamber of Commerce in Australia
53 Martin Place, 9th Floor
Sydney, N.S.W. 2000, Australia
Phone: 233.6177
Cable: AMCHAM SYDNEY
Telex: 22792

Branch Offices

Lee Cannon, Adelaide Manager
American Chamber of Commerce in Australia
8th Floor, 50 Grenfell Street
Adelaide, S.A. 5000, Australia
Phone: 87 5781

Inge O'Brien, Brisbane Manager
American Chamber of Commerce in Australia
4th Floor, Combined Insurance House
139 Leichhardt Street
Brisbane, Queensland 4000, Australia
Phone: 221 8542

C. C. Miller, Melbourne Manager
American Chamber of Commerce in Australia
3rd Floor, 186 Exhibition Street
Melbourne, Victoria 3000, Australia
Phone: 662 3535

Pat Maxwell, Perth Manager
American Chamber of Commerce
in Australia
9th Floor, 16 St. George's Terrace
Perth, W. A. 6000, Australia
Phone: 25 9540

Austria

Dr. Patricia A. Helletzgruber,
Manager
American Chamber of Commerce
in Austria
Severingasse 1
A-1090 Vienna, Austria
Phone: 41 12 71
Cable: USACHAMBER
Telex: 013711

Belgium

Wayne Fisher, Executive Director
The American Chamber of
Commerce in Belgium
Rue du Commerce 21
B-1040, Brussels, Belgium
Phone: (02) 512 12 62

Brazil, Rio de Janeiro

Augusto De Moura Diniz, Jr.
Executive Vice President
The American Chamber of
Commerce for Brazil
Av. Rio Branco 123
Rio de Janeiro, Brazil
Phone: 222-1983
Cable: AMERCHACOM

Branch Office

M. S. de Azevedo, Executive
Secretary
The American Chamber of
Commerce for Brazil
Caixa Postal 3351
30.000 Recife, Pernambuco, Brazil
Phone: 245988

Brazil, Sao Paulo

Executive Director (Vacant)
American Chamber of Commerce
for Brazil
P.O. Box 8109
01000 São Paulo, Brazil
Phone: 37-7181/4
Cable: AMERCHACOM

Branch Office

Regina Muller, Executive Secretary
The American Chamber of
Commerce for Brazil
P.O. Box 1572
90.000 Porto Alegre, Brazil
Phone: 25-0356/0512
Cable: AMERCHACOM

Chile

Bernard J. Curtis, Secretary
The Chamber of Commerce of the
U.S.A. in the Republic of Chile
Casilla 4131
Santiago, Chile
Phone: 86348
Cable: AMCHAMBER

China, Republic of

Herbert Gale Peabody, Executive
Director
The Taipei-American Chamber of
Commerce
P.O. Box 17-277
Taipei, Republic of China
Phone: 552515
Cable: AMCHAM TAIPEI
Telex: 21705

Colombia

Oscar A. Bradford, President
Colombian-American Chamber of
Commerce
Hotel Bogotá Hilton, #701
Bogotá, D.E., Colombia
Phone: 329701
Cable: CAMCOLAM BOGOTA
Telex: 044326

Branch Office

Maria Cecilia Monsalve Cabal
Executive Director
Colombian-American Chamber of Commerce
Apartado 5943
Cali, Valle, Colombia
Phone: 77 10 12

Costa Rica

Felicia M. Morales, Manager
The American Chamber of Commerce of Costa Rica
Apartado Postal 4946
San José, Costa Rica
Phone: 23 24 97
Cable: AMCHAM
Telex: 2197

Dominican Republic

Maximo E. Velazquez, Executive Director
The American Chamber of Commerce of the Dominican Republic
P.O. Box 95-2
Hotel El Embajador
Santo Domingo, Dominican Republic
Phone: 533-7292
Cable: AMCHAM
Telex: 3460010 (ITT)

Ecuador

Karl Newlands, Executive Director
Camara de Comercio Ecuatoriano-Americana
Apartado 2432
Quito, Ecuador
Phone: 543-512
Cable: ECUAME
Telex: 2298

El Salvador

William Chinchilla, Manager
American Chamber of Commerce of El Salvador
Apartado Postal (05) 9
San Salvador, El Salvador
Phone: 23-6056
Cable: AMCHAM

France

W. Barrett Dower, Executive Director
The American Chamber of Commerce in France
21, Avenue George V
Paris 75008, France
Phone: 225 01 54
Cable: AMCHAM
Telex: 65021

Germany

Paul G. Baudler, Executive Secretary
The American Chamber of Commerce in Germany
Rossmarkt 12
6000 Frankfurt/Main, Germany
Phone: (0611) 28 34 01
Cable: AMECOC

Branch Offices

Robert H. Lochner, Representative
The American Chamber of Commerce in Germany
Fasanenstrasse 4
1000 Berlin 12, Germany
Phone: (030) 31 70 01
Cable: AMA SCOT BERLIN

Fr. Dr. D. Noltenius, Representative
The American Chamber of Commerce in Germany
Haus der Handelskammer Bremen
Hinter dem Schuetting
2800 Bremen, Germany
Phone: (0421) 35371

Gunter Mayer-Rolshoven, Representative
The American Chamber of Commerce in Germany
Wirmerstrasse 11
4000 Dusseldorf 30, Germany
Phone: (0211) 435600

Dr. Leo M. Goodman, Representative
The American Chamber of Commerce in Germany
Zweibruckenstrasse 6
8000 Munich 22, Germany
Phone: (0811) 295953

Guatemala

B. W. Rudder, Executive Manager
The American Chamber of Commerce of Guatemala
Apartado No. 832
9ª Calle 5-54, Zona 1
Guatemala City, Guatemala
Phone: 82-020
Cable: AMCHAM GUATAMELACITY

Hong Kong

Herbert L. Minich, Executive Director
The American Chamber of Commerce in Hong Kong
322 Edinburgh House
Hong Kong
Phone: 5-260165
Cable: AMCHAM
Telex: 73446

Indonesia

The American Business Group of Indonesia
P.O. Box 2086
Djakarta, Indonesia
Phone: 56288/56284
Cable: DARALON
Telex: 46279

Iran

Irwin C. Nye, Executive Director
The Iran-American Chamber of Commerce
7th Floor, Iranian's Bank Building
Takhte Jamshid Avenue
Tehran 15, Iran
Phone: 834320
Cable: IRANAMCHAM TEHRAN

Ireland

Robert P. Chalker, Executive Director
U.S. Chamber of Commerce in Ireland
16 Eustace Street
Dublin 2, Ireland
Phone: 775554
Cable: AMCHAM DUBLIN
Telex: 5795

Italy

Herman H. Burdick, General Secretary
American Chamber of Commerce in Italy
Via Agnello 12
20121 Milan, Italy
Phone: 807955/6
Cable: AMERCAM

Branch Office

Susan K. Stanfield, Secretary
American Chamber of Commerce in Italy
Via Lombardia 40
00187 Rome, Italy
Phone: 4754540

Japan

W. Bart Jackson, Executive Director
The American Chamber of Commerce in Japan
701 Tosho Building
3-2-2 Marunouchi, 3-chome
Chiyoda-ku, Tokyo 100, Japan
Phone: (03) 211-5861/3
Cable: AMERCHAM

Japan, Okinawa

Col. William H. Nelson, Jr., Executive Director
The American Chamber of Commerce in Okinawa
Manneng Bldg., 136 Oyama, Ginowan Shi
Okinawa-Ken, Japan 901-22
Phone: 09889-7-2118
Cable: AMCHAM
Telex: 79856

Korea

Charles W. Semple, Executive Director
The American Chamber of Commerce in Korea
3rd Floor, Chosun Hotel
Seoul, Korea
Phone: 23-6471
Cable: AMCHAMBER
Telex: 2349

Mexico

Al R. Wichtrich, Executive Vice President
The American Chamber of Commerce of Mexico
Lucerna 78, A.P. 82 BIS
Mexico 6, D.F., Mexico
Phone: 566-0866
Cable: AMCHAMMEX
Telex: 01772434

Branch Offices

Gilbert E. Larsen, General Manager
The American Chamber of Commerce of Mexico
16 de Septiembre 730-301
Guadalajara, Jalisco, Mexico
Phone: 12-26-49
Cable: AMCHAMMEX

Lic. Ricardo Maiz Garcia, Manager
The American Chamber of Commerce of Mexico
Condominio Acero, Desp. 213
Monterrey, Nuevo Leon, Mexico
Phone: 44-00-90
Cable: AMCHAMMEX

Morocco

Gladys M. Levy, Executive Secretary
The American Chamber of Commerce in Morocco
Hotel El Mansour
27 Avenue de l'Armee Royale
Casablanca, Morocco
Phone: 22-14-48
Cable: AMCHAM
Telex: 21728

Netherlands

Adriana J. van der Graaf, General Manager
The American Chamber of Commerce in the Netherlands
Carnegieplein 5
The Hague, The Netherlands
Phone: 070-659808
Cable: AMCHAM
Telex: 31542

New Zealand

Harry A. Purcell, Executive Manager
American Chamber of Commerce in New Zealand
P.O. Box 3408
Wellington, New Zealand
Phone: 43-793
Telex: 3514 (for AmCham)

Nicaragua

Oscar Stadthagen, Executive Director
American Chamber of Commerce of Nicaragua
Apartado 2720
Managua, Nicaragua
Phone: 8765-8796
Cable: AMCHAM

Peru

Romeo Cubas, Manager
The American Chamber of Commerce of Peru
P.O. Box 2888
Lima 1, Peru
Phone: 403-425
Cable: AMCHAMPERU
Telex: 25643

Philippine Islands

Lt. Gen. Jesus M. Vargas AFP (Ret.)
Executive Vice President
American Chamber of Commerce of the Philippines
P.O. Box 1836
Manila, The Philippines
Phone: 86-51-15
Cable: AMCHAMCOM

Singapore

John A. Siniscal, Honorary Secretary
American Business Council of Singapore
1st Floor, Yen San Building
268 Orchard Road
Singapore 9
Phone: 350077
Telex: 21561

Spain

Brigham G. Day, Executive Director
The American Chamber of Commerce in Spain
Avda. Generalissimo Franco 477
Barcelona 11, Spain
Phone: 321 81 95/96
Cable: AMCHAM

Branch Office

John S. Fitzpatrick, Staff Officer
The American Chamber of Commerce in Spain
Hotel Eurobuilding
Padre Damian 23
Madrid 14, Spain
Phone: 4586520
Cable: AMCHAM
Telex: 22548

Switzerland

Walter H. Diggelmann, Executive Director
Swiss-American Chamber of Commerce
Talacker 41
8001 Zurich, Switzerland
Phone: (01) 27 24 55
Cable: AMCHAMBER
Telex: 53448

Thailand

Jack Scott, Executive Director
The American Chamber of Commerce in Thailand
P.O. Box 11-1095
Bangkok, Thailand
Phone: 519266
Cable: Amercham
Telex: 2778 (for AmCham)

United Kingdom

Jack A. Herfurt, Director General
The American Chamber of Commerce (United Kingdom)
75 Brook Street
London W1Y 2EB, England
Phone: 01 4930381
Cable: AMCHAM LONDON W1

Uruguay

John L. Micheloni, Manager
The Chamber of Commerce of the U.S.A. in Uruguay
P.O. Box 389
Montevideo, Uruguay
Phone: 86052
Cable: AMCHAM
Telex: 3918419 (ITT)

Venezuela

Dr. Frank J. Amador, Executive Director
Venezuelan-American Chamber of Commerce and Industry
Apartado 5181
Caracas, D.F., Venezuela
Phone: 912-366
Cable: AMBERCO

OTHER WORTHWHILE CONTACTS AND TACTICS

Other worthwhile contacts in foreign lands are professional societies and social groups such as the Lions and Rotary Clubs. On one occasion in Rio de Janeiro, I met several of the people I wanted to see at the Rio Yacht Club at a social gathering. The Rio Yacht Club happened to be affiliated with my own here on Chesapeake Bay. At another time in Bogotá, Colombia, I decided to play tennis (at 8,700 feet above sea level) in order to chance a get-together with one particularly difficult official who could not be reached through his office. He later became a very good client and trusted personal friend. Visits to the local university may lead to an offer to give a talk to the graduating class or an impromptu discussion on a subject of technical interest with local intellectuals: all these are examples of the kind of tactics that I have found effective when it was time to zero in.

Press conferences, cocktail parties, and sumptuous dinners nowadays do little to generate business; they do not enhance a professional reputation and image, except under very special circumstances. Invitations with key personnel for a breakfast meeting or a business luncheon, however, are frequently accepted and serve a more useful purpose.

There is no doubt that it takes considerable patience, experience, and a somewhat outgoing personality to get close enough to a prospective client so that an initial consultant-to-client relationship is born. It certainly cannot be done on a nine-to-five domestic schedule. International consultants have to recognize that their clients use different standards to measure their proposed mentors. Frequently, several written submissions are requested prior to shortlisting and the consultants' reaction to time-delaying exercises is closely scrutinized. To zero in successfully, much may well depend on a patient and thoughtful initial "courtship."

Bankers everywhere are usually well informed and easily accessible. The nature of their business obliges them to be fully aware of what is going on locally, nationally, and regionally. They communicate well among themselves and with others. Whenever I need a quick appraisal of a new market, I visit one or two banks and request a meeting with the ranking official. Over the years, I have found that local banks frequently have close ties with the authorities and are in the position to arrange for interviews. Branches of the large international banks are frequently better informed of the overall political and economic conditions. Thus, I usually try to visit with at least one each to obtain the benefits of full coverage. One word of caution in dealing with bankers may be in order: There does not exist the doctor-to-patient or lawyer-to-client relationship in commercial banking. It is quite possible, therefore, that information given a banker is passed on to competitors. Good judgment has to be used, and discretion may have to be exercised during initial meetings. On the other hand, once a banking relationship has been established, and the importance of confidentiality of a certain project is understood by the bank, there should be less reason for restraint.

Major banks all over the world are interconnected and maintain lines of credit among each other. Anybody going abroad into new territories may do well to inquire at home with the banker who handles his daily business about correspondents at the point of destination. A letter of introduction from one banker to another opens many doors. Consequently, an indication to the manager of a foreign bank that he may well be chosen to handle the consultant's account if the job comes through will do even more.

CONCLUSION

The process of spotting and then zeroing in on foreign prospects is a difficult and challenging one. It requires a special kind of spirit, tenacity, tact, and strength of character. To identify a forthcoming undertaking and then to maneuver in a professional manner in order to become the client's choice to perform professional services with the expenditure of reasonable costs is a most gratifying accomplishment for any international consultant.

PREPARING PROPOSALS FOR OVERSEAS WORK

Writing and editing, translating into one or more foreign languages, printing and binding, and finally delivering and following through a proposal for professional services is a significant undertaking. Additionally, this effort requires a heavy investment in time and expenditures. Consultants should be aware of the fact that a first-class international proposal fully backed up with supporting data and documentation may cost thousands of dollars and, therefore, must be regarded as a major new business development investment.

In view of the high cost of such an undertaking, it is only prudent to carefully examine one's chances for success. A number of basic questions ought to be answered in the affirmative before proceeding with the main work for a proposal.

- Does the prospective client command sufficient financial means to pay for the required services?
- Is the area in which the project is planned politically stable and economically sound?
- Are foreign consultants welcome? Is the record of past international performance and acceptance in the host country a favorable one?
- Are we reasonably sure that our services as foreign consultants in general and our firm in particular will be considered, and are we welcome?
- Do they really need us? How many competitors will we face?

- Is the geographical area of the proposed works one that is of real interest to us?
- Do we have the expertise to compete successfully against other consultants from our own and from other countries, who may be among the best in the world?
- Do we have staff available and interested in working overseas? Are we financially capable of handling the job?

Many years ago, attending a meeting of the venerable Export Managers Council of New York, a respected old gentleman explained that in his line of business of electrical construction materials, the main concern was to get as many proposals out into the international marketplace as possible because the records indicated that his firm received a steady flow of orders, amounting to a return of something like 15 or 20 percent of proposals submitted. This may have been true in olden days and for the export of goods. It certainly does not apply to proposals covering the performance of professional services overseas.

As mentioned in other chapters of this book, it is a combination of good international intelligence, sound management, in-depth professional expertise, administrative flexibility, and financial independence that provides the basis for profitable international engagements. Preparing proposals for overseas work, therefore, has to be done selectively and with a great deal of care.

International consultants perform a large variety of tasks. Proposals may be limited to prefeasibility and investment studies, preliminary design and cost estimates, definitive design and specifications, supervision of construction or construction management, training of host-country nationals, education, health, economics, and management of old and new facilities. Additionally, it is not at all unusual for an international consultant to submit unsolicited proposals for professional services. We cannot, therefore, discuss in this book all the varying factors and conditions that need to be considered for each and every proposal. However, the following will describe in some detail the basic components of customary proposal documents.

INTRODUCTION

The very first part of any proposal should be a brief letter to the prospective client, making reference to the Request for Proposal (RFP) or any specific circumstances that motivated the particular presentation. It is of singular importance that this introductory letter be properly directed to the right party, correctly addressed, and fully referenced. Consultants should be careful with the spelling of foreign names and the use of titles and degrees in the proposed host country and—beware—with foreign addresses. I know of one technically impressive proposal that was discarded without consideration by a foreign government entity simply because a title had been omitted and the name of a minister misspelled.

INTRODUCING THE COMPANY

A consultant will have to use judgment as to how much detail is required to properly introduce his firm to the prospective client. If the firm has worked in the area and is known by its past performance, the introduction may obviously be quite brief. On the other hand, if it is a first attempt to enter into a new country, it definitely is in the consultant's best interest to tell as much about his firm as he can.

A number of consultants have developed brochures and generally descriptive illustrated material covering the past and current activities of their organization. The reader may be interested to note that in a few foreign countries, these publications are regarded as "picture books," at best, and that the contents thereof will not be taken into consideration when the official scoreboard is being filled. There have been too many cases of firms, small and large, who all claim to have planned, designed, and built New York City's Empire State Building, San Francisco's Golden Gate Bridge, the Hoover Dam, etc. If a consultant's story is to be told, it should appear in the introductory chapter with, perhaps, reference to printed material attached, but still outlining the most important points that should come across to the selection official or board.

An overseas client is principally interested in the age of the organization, its ownership, size, and activities. It may be useful to present the firm in general terms first, and then to dedicate space to overseas experience in general and in the particular international area to which the proposal is directed. Few professionals have worked everywhere in the world and foreign clients know this; therefore, do not exaggerate claims about overseas experience. Too many references to the personal involvement of one or the other firm's employees in particular international engagements should also be avoided. Consulting work, after all, requires skill in team management and adaptability to varying circumstances. The ability to express this in a straightforward and honest way will score higher than unsubstantiable claims of past experience and questionable area knowledge.

It may be well, under certain circumstances, to accompany a proposal with a copy of the registration form that has been filed with one of the international financial institutions or development agencies, if the project is expected to be financed by one of these. In other cases, it may suffice merely to mention that the firm is on record with these institutions. In any event, a first introduction should also include a few outstanding, reputable references, such as important international clients (if available), prominent domestic or multinational connections, and at least one solid banking reference. For the latter, while for instance the First National Bank & Trust Company of Darling, Montana, may be an excellent bank, it is certainly better to provide the name of one of the large international banking houses that are known worldwide.

TERMS OF REFERENCE AND SCOPE OF WORK

Requests for proposals frequently contain terms of reference that are vague, incomplete, and sometimes even contradictory. Other times, however, RFPs are excellent in every respect and could not be any clearer. In every case, a consulting firm should spare no time and effort in reviewing what is requested in the invitation and coming forward with a proposal containing the scope of work and terms of reference written in the consultant's own words. When a prospective client carefully reviews a number of proposals, he will quickly note who has copied his original language verbatim and who has presented a "fully responsive" offering; my experience is that he is usually much more impressed when a consultant might differ in terms of reference and scope of work, as it does demonstrate not only a thoughtful approach, but independent professional thinking. Terms of reference and the scope of work will almost always be the subject of extensive discussions during the negotiations that follow acceptance of a proposal; therefore, a consultant is always on firm ground when he expands or limits his initial response to this crucial subject. For large proposed undertakings, it may be well to propose alternate approaches, or to phase the proposed work into various stages.

Whenever the wording of the proposal is different from that of the RFP, it is recommended that a paragraph be written into the proposal to the effect that the final terms of reference and the scope of work are subject to mutual agreement during negotiations. A number of foreign clients make it a rule to include the proposal as an accompanying document with the final contract because in case of misunderstandings leading to disputes, this paragraph could be a lifesaver.

SCHEDULES

Sophisticated foreign clients, and there are more and more of these nowadays, will include their own scheduling of the works and the completion dates that they desire. Once again, just as we discussed above in the case of the terms of reference and the scope of work, a consultant must review these most carefully. He must take into account not only the firm's ability to meet the proposed schedules, but also such circumstances as dry and rainy seasons in the tropics, religious and other holidays in certain areas, the number of people and entities who are to participate in the project or to review stages thereof, and other factors over which the consultant has little or no control. Simple matters of logistics, such as obtaining visas and work permits for personnel, import licenses for equipment, and local transport from port of entry to the job site are important relative to scheduling work.

In Guatemala City at one time, I was told by members of the highway department that they had little difficulty in selecting only the really experienced of several unknown consulting firms. They accomplished this simply by scrutinizing the proposed schedules submitted for a highway feasibility study several hundred miles away from the coast, in the rain forests of the Peten Region. It was the firm that had taken into account such matters as jungle clearing during the dry season, mobilization via river transportation at the end of the rainy season, and, most importantly, the need to get to and from the job site through a third country, that was awarded the opportunity to negotiate a contract.

There is nothing wrong with a realistic "consultant's schedule," but outside factors must be anticipated and should be noted. These should definitely include the client's obligations to contribute his share of the work within the stipulated time.

International engagements do not start up as promptly and as easily as the average domestic ones. Delays that can be foreseen should be incorporated in the schedule as early as the time of submitting a proposal. Additional delays do come up more often than not. Instead of following the domestic practice of scheduling calendar days, weeks, months, etc., overseas work requires the use of bar graphs showing the various stages and completion dates in days, weeks, or months after start-up. If there is a factor of seasons involved, then it may be wise to submit alternate schedules in order to cover eventualities.

Time is most important to every client and for every job. All jobs should have been started up yesterday in order to be completed tomorrow. Proposals are not normally judged entirely on the basis of scheduling; but a consultant who shows understanding and a realistic attitude toward the client's needs might place himself ahead of his competitors by paying careful attention to this particular detail.

In this connection, it has been my experience that if a consultant has expressed a willingness to waive certain conditions prior to mobilization, he may be placed ahead of his competitors in the final selection process. For instance, if the reputation and the credit of the client is unquestionable, a consultant may well agree to mobilize immediately following the signing of the agreement or the ratification thereof. The start-up, hence, could occur prior to the receipt of an irrevocable, confirmed letter of credit (LC). These payment documents need time to come through, particularly if third parties, such as international financiers, are involved. Likewise, if agreements and contracts are subject to review and approvals and if the consultant is willing to assume the risk that the conditions will not be questioned, he can offer to proceed ahead of time. Such gestures, in a formal proposal, are rarely overlooked and often appreciated. They may substantially contribute toward the desired outcome, namely the award of a contract.

PROPOSED EXECUTION OF THE ENGAGEMENT

It is not often than an RFP will detail how a consulting firm is to proceed with the execution of professional performance. This is usually left to the executing firm. And it is here that considerable effort should be given to the proposal, as it will show the full extent of the consultant's understanding of the task ahead and may even be the factor in helping the client to decide that the selected approach is indeed in the best interest of the project. Is the job to be done in the host country or at the consultant's home office? What are the various steps that are proposed to be taken and in what order? How much support will be requested from the client, or how independent does the consultant propose to be? What standards are going to be followed? Will the reports be submitted in more than one language and, say, in metric measurements? Will specifications be issued for international bidding according to the rules and regulations of any particular financial institution or development agency?

These and, of course, a good many other observations should complement the schedule and the scope of work, to be followed in turn by a discussion of associations, joint ventures, partnerships, and subcontracts.

ASSOCIATIONS, SUBCONTRACTS, JOINT VENTURES

Within the context of the discussion of proposals, a consultant should explain to the prospective client his established policy in these matters. Some countries demand participation of their own nationals in all engineering and construction projects. This may have to be substantiated by including a letter of agreement to the effect that a local firm or individual has agreed to render specific services. Such a letter will confirm to the client that this condition of the RFP is clearly understood and followed. In such a case, it may be necessary, as a matter of fact, to include references, past history and experience, etc., of the local firm into the general proposal.

Selecting competent and capable local assistance for the execution of professional services is particularly difficult, especially when the time to submit a proposal is short. For some who have worked in the area overseas and who have permanent connections, it represents no great obstacle, but others may find this one of the most difficult parts of responding to a RFP. When facing this kind of a situation, I have on occasion been successful by writing into the proposal that local associates, as required, would be selected either prior to the start-up of negotiations or after receipt of advice that the proposal has been accepted. I have even been able to convince the client that host-country employees or associates would be selected *after* the conclusive negotiation of a contract, subject to the client's approval. In this latter case, I have actually benefited from the client's knowledge of available professionals. Once in a while a situation develops in which nonprofessional political or personal considerations thus threaten to enter, but these can usually be tactfully disposed of without causing serious damage. The overall purpose of subcontracts, associations, and joint ventures is to satisfy the client as to the proposed approach and to avoid being disqualified because of having overlooked a factor which is of increasing importance to host-country customers in the emerging nations. See Chapter 8, "Associations, Joint Ventures, Representation," for a more detailed discussion.

STAFFING

Recently, in discussing the work of selection committees in one of the large international development banks with a group of consulting engineers, a ranking bank official said that consulting-contract awards are rated with the heaviest emphasis on the proposed project manager and field personnel. He went into considerable detail to explain that the project manager must not be the president of the company, the executive vice president of the international division, or the general representative of the company in the contract area. The project manager is the person who is directly in charge and is responsible for the execution of the assignment. This is what the experienced client is looking for more than anything else. International consultants, of course, are not ignorant of the importance of having their best available employee in charge of an overseas project, and it is quite customary to propose first-class project managers wherever and whenever possible. One of the great difficulties in an international practice, however, is the fact that it may take weeks and months before a proposal is accepted and negotiated and all the conditions precedent to start-up are fulfilled. By that time, the project manager who has been listed may have long been engaged elsewhere, left the firm, or even retired from the demanding work of an overseas team manager. Therefore, the designation of a specific project manager is difficult, to say the least. International consultants, after submitting the names and biographies of several of their project managers, should write into the proposal that one of these, or others with equivalent qualifications, will be assigned, preferentially, of course, to the client's choice, if available at the time of mobilization. If the client, in his RFP, insists on designating specific individuals for positions, then the consultant may have to stipulate that the proposal naming personnel is valid only for a certain number of weeks or months. It is recognized that it is impossible, of course, to hold valuable people in reserve indefinitely. With the amount of international work and the number of proposals that are submitted by international consultants these days, it will also be likely that the same person is proposed as project manager for several jobs in various areas. This should also be made quite clear to the prospective client, and the same applies, to a somewhat lesser degree, to other members of the team who are proposed to be directly involved in the field.

The preparation of the biographies of the project manager and field personnel is important. As mentioned above, this is where the closest scrutiny may be expected. The rise and fall of a consultant's proposal is more closely related to the selection of the proposed project manager and field staff than to anything else.

It should not be overlooked, however, that field staff has to be supported from the home office and that headquarters staff must properly back up the field with technical and logistical assistance. Therefore, while it is not necessary to list very many people in addition to the field personnel, it is good policy to detail who will be involved from the home front and to back up these names with detailed matter-of-fact biographies.

VISUAL AIDS

When large projects are being scheduled, a consulting firm may be well advised to provide not only a bar graph showing the proposed timing for the execution of works, but also organizational charts showing the overall company organization, international setup, and the proposed organization for the project. Such charts should be supported by copies of company policy memoranda, explaining how the firm operates overseas. This material need not be prepared specifically for each proposal and every client; it is something that an international consultant should have ready for any event. I will discuss some of these in Chapter 5, "Staffing for Multinational Engagements."

COMPENSATION

Consultants' fees for professional services are negotiated internationally in a manner somewhat similar to domestic U.S. procedures. It is certainly not advisable to include any kind of a fee until such a time as word is received that the proposal has been accepted subject to mutually satisfactory agreement of conditions of contract.

From time to time, RFPs include requests for details or man-hour estimates, the compensation of various classifications of personnel, and other information that would enable an experienced client to estimate approximate costs. I am not averse to furnishing this information, as long as the terms of reference and the scope of work are sufficiently detailed to permit reasonable estimates of man-hour involvement, etc. At other times, when less-experienced clients request cost information after providing incomplete terms of reference and scope of work, it may be necessary to indicate that fees are established according to the required input of man-hours, expenses, the firm's overhead, and a reasonable profit, all of which can be substantiated only after discussions at the negotiating table.

It certainly serves neither the client's nor the consultant's purpose to volunteer compensation, fees, and other cost figures in a proposal. However, it is quite in order and can be a plus for the final award considerations if there is a sentence to the effect that full disclosure of all costs will be made during negotiations and that the consulting firm is maintaining books and records in accordance with established procedures and is willing to submit to audit. Chapter 4, "Negotiating Contracts Abroad," addresses itself in detail to fee considerations as far as proposals are concerned.

DRAFT CONTRACTS

Lately, a number of RFPs have appeared with a requirement that a proposal include a draft contract. This is not an unreasonable demand, and an international consultant should oblige. The proposal should be accompanied by a form of agreement that incorporates the body of the proposal but leaves open such matters as parts of the terms of reference, scope of work, scheduling, compensation, special conditions, etc., which can only be agreed upon during negotiations. It should be clearly understood that a draft contract is not a binding document, but simply a proposal that incorporates the consultant's customary overseas policies and conditions. According to the sophistication and experience of the client, a firm may go into some detail as to which other conditions, in addition to the ones mentioned above, can be subject to special negotiations.

LANGUAGE

I have often been asked if a proposal should be prepared in the client's or in the consultant's language. My immediate answer is always, "Both." I firmly believe that a client is entitled to have the consultant work with him in his language, and if there is a question of one language only, I think it is, with rare exceptions, the client's language that should prevail.

A good, sound, technically proficient, and well-translated (or well-written) foreign language proposal goes a long way toward establishing claims of language proficiency. Let there be no doubt, language proficiency will have to be confirmed later on during personal meetings.

When a host-country client and a third-country international financial agency are involved, proposals may be subject to review and acceptance by both. In this case, more than one language may be requested and required for the successful proponent. Unless the proposal document is particularly voluminous and heavy, I recommend that translations appear on opposite pages and not in separate binders or books. It is easier to work with multiple languages by having these combined in the same volume. Also, it facilitates ready reference to details in translations, minimizing the possibility of errors which occur so easily. When preparing proposal documents in a foreign language and in English, a consultant may have to look for translation facilities and presses outside his normal area of operations. International firms generally try to maintain permanent and up-to-date files on technical and commercial translators and printers in various areas of the world where work is performed or assignments are expected to come up.

One more word about translations: The spoken French of a Canadian is not the same as that of a Haitian. But the written French is similar and acceptable. The spoken Spanish of a Cuban is comprehended in Colombia and in Chile. However, the written Spanish of a Cuban will be rejected by a Colombian as erratic, and by a Chilean as hard to understand. There are many more examples that I could cite. International firms must be careful in the selection of their translators when negotiating agreements, writing contracts, and submitting reports. The first indication to a prospective client of how well the consultant works in his language is evident in the proposal. A professional service proposal needs to be handled by a technical translator, not a college language professor or a student from a foreign country who wants to earn extra income.

THE MAKE-UP OF A PROPOSAL

In Indonesia a couple of years ago, a high government official complained to me that he had received a dozen volumes, each containing nearly 100 pages and a great many pictures, when the proposals therein could have simply been presented with a twenty-page letter and a copy of a registration form from the World Bank. Only a few months later, in Peru, an indignant minister of public works pointed out to me that one foreign consultant had dared to submit a proposal for professional service in a twenty-page letter, while others had presented handsomely bound books with his name imprinted in gold on the cover. It follows that there exists no hard and fast rule that can be followed. If the deciding vote for the award of a contract positively rests with only one individual, the consultant may enhance his chance to be selected by catering to the client's taste. In the vast majority of cases, however, it is advisable to prepare a no-nonsense, detailed proposal similar in form and shape to the format of reports that are customarily presented to all the consultant's domestic and foreign clients.

A proposal presentation may also contain samples of work that the firm has performed. However, consideration must be given to the fact that not all nations maintain friendly relations among themselves. For instance, to use an industrial feasibility report for an Israeli installation to support a proposal for similar works in Libya, at this time at least, would be disastrous. In addition, many foreign clients require that their reports be kept strictly confidential. Hence, samples of work that are submitted to support proposals must be authorized and cleared for the purpose of the promotion of new business for the consultant.

PREPARATORY FIELD VISITS

I firmly believe that, at one time or another, prior to the "opening of the proposals" by the client, the consultant should make a personal appearance in the host country. Most of the time, it is more beneficial to do so in order to gather pertinent information for the project and to write into the proposal that the consultant has become familiar with local requirements and conditions, having been there. In some cases, if local translation and printing schedules can be arranged, it may be more convenient to visit the host country shortly before the time of the proposal presentation. At that time it may be well worth the consultant's time to stay over a day or two and substantiate the firm's seriousness with a demonstration—by personally delivering the proposal and, of course, identifying himself and his firm in the process. Some countries have rules and regulations whereby professional proposals are received like bids from contractors by an official of the public administration, who issues a written receipt. Others simply stipulate that the document must be received at a certain ministry, not later than a certain date and time, and that it must be addressed to a ranking official. In the first case, obviously, a personal presentation could be a waste of time. In the latter, it might be useful to inject the personal contact.

THE PRESENTATION

In conclusion, after a firm has spent many man-hours in preparing a proposal, used expensive translation services, and printed a costly proposal document, the idea of investing an additional thousand dollars or so in a personal presentation is tempting and should not be rejected outright. In some cases, the decision comes easily. Every so often, proposal preparations fall behind in schedule and the only sure way to get the documentation to the client on time is to hand it over personally. But, in the majority of cases, timely air-freighting or air-mailing of the proposal or having a local friend, associate, or representative deliver the documentation in person is satisfactory. Yet it is unwise to blindly trust one's good luck and simply hope for the best.

When proposing to perform professional services for private enterprise, it is a relatively easy matter to judge the importance of presenting a proposal personally or having it delivered through the mails or third parties. There is only one rule that stands up in practically every case: Whenever an official entity is involved, the review time for a proposal will be long—considerably longer than that of private industry.

From my personal experience over many years, I would say that I feel more at ease when I know that my firm's proposal has been personally presented by somebody fully representing our interests.

NEGOTIATING CONTRACTS ABROAD

It is always good to hear that the client has decided to negotiate an agreement. A number of conclusions are obvious: We have effectively selected a certain geographical area in which to perform professional services. Our proposal has been of definite interest to the client. The general form of our presentation and its contents inspired the confidence that we can do the job. Our technical expertise and general qualifications were good enough to secure the invitation to negotiate. In short, we have done our basic homework.

THE PREPARATIONS (AT HOME)

The next step is to draw up a contract that covers the client's needs, secures the consultant's requirements, and, when necessary, satisfies interested third parties, such as the international financial agencies and development institutions that may have an interest in the project.

I remember the days prior to World War II when I was once shown some banana plantations by the client, the United Fruit Company of Guatemala. Shortly after the visit I received a letter commissioning me to specify and design "adequate irrigation." This same letter, in two sentences, established my fee and the time of delivery. The whole document was less than one typewritten page.

Times have changed. Certain projects are still quite simple, but procedures have become more sophisticated and, of course, the large international engagements today are highly complex, deeply involved, and often require expertise in many professional fields including the environmental and social sciences. Contracts, therefore, can be expected to be extremely complicated and detailed. Despite more than thirty years of experience in international work, I find today that I still come across questions for which I do not have an immediate answer and for which I need information from the home office or outsiders, despite all preparations. I do not hesitate to admit this to my prospective clients. Nothing is more detrimental than to pretend to know it all, and then to be caught ignorant at a crucial time. It is best to be prepared as well as possible from the very beginning.

Generally, nowadays, the negotiation of a contract covering professional services is not a routine process, even within the United States, where there has existed a previous consultant-client relationship. Overseas, all engagements require careful analysis, thorough discussions, and a clear understanding of everything that can be anticipated and should be covered.

Over the years, I have spent much more time in preparing for negotiations than in sitting across the conference table and hammering out acceptable terms and conditions. Specifically, there are four main areas that require extensive homework: (1) scope of work, (2) general conditions, (3) compensation and conditions of payment, and (4) special conditions.

Several of the procedures and items discussed in the following paragraphs are mentioned in greater detail in the other chapters of this book. However, it may be useful to have ready reference available within the context of "negotiating contracts abroad."

Scope of Work

From a technical point of view it is imperative to have a full, mutual understanding as to the job requirements and to have these spelled out in as much detail as possible. Inasmuch as the scope of work determines what the consultant has to provide, it automatically lays the groundwork for the work plan, schedules, and personnel that will be involved in the execution of the engagement and in the compensation.

General Conditions

The second area is the so-called general conditions. Is it proposed to undertake all the work in-house or will there be subcontracts? What kind of progress reports are required? Will books and records be needed for inspection and auditing purposes overseas and at our home office? What are the times of commencement and completion? How can the agreement be terminated for valid reasons either by the client or the consultant? What constitutes force majeure? How may possible disputes be settled? Can the contract be assigned to a third party? Is there need to protect the ownership of processes and the rights of studies, plans, and specifications? These general conditions exist in almost all professional agreements and can be put together with relative ease, after some experience in overseas work.

Compensation

The third, and perhaps the most complicated area requiring extensive preparation is that of compensation and conditions of payment. As a first observation, I might mention that any fee may be regarded as unreasonable and too high unless the client fully understands what it represents. On the other hand, fees can be too low if the scope of work is not specifically defined and sufficiently tied together with the general conditions and the special conditions that form part of the basic agreement.

Regardless of the type of compensation that is contemplated (lump sum, time charge, direct salary plus a percentage, or percentage of construction cost—just to mention a few), the consultant must be in the position to clearly indicate how the fee approach is structured and how the total compensation can be justified.

The establishment of fair and equitable compensation always demands much thought and a complete comprehension of the contracting process. However, for an overseas contract there are numerous additional factors that must be taken into consideration, as they make fee calculations more complicated. The following table provides a guideline to international fee estimates:

A GUIDELINE TO INTERNATIONAL FEE ESTIMATES

1. *Job-Related (Direct) Time Cost*
   - Home office personnel
   - Expatriate staff located overseas
   - Local employees
   - Third-country nationals
   - Others

A GUIDELINE TO INTERNATIONAL FEE ESTIMATES (Continued)

2. *Job-Related (Direct) Expense Cost*
   Transportation (international and domestic)
   Per diems
   Living, transportation (local), education
   Office rental, camp facilities
   Vehicles, equipment, furniture
   Local vacations
   Special insurance
   Miscellaneous

3. *Overhead*

4. *Subcontracts and Outside Services*

5. *Local Costs*
   Taxes, registration, import duties, work permits
   Translations
   Drivers, guards, interpreters
   Legal counsel

6. *Escalation of Time and Expense Costs*

7. *Contingency*

8. *Profit*

Note: Each item should be fully substantiated by detailed back-up calculations.

Now, let us look at some of the basics that must be taken into consideration.

Direct-Time Costs

First of all, it is necessary to estimate the direct-time cost for all personnel involved in the execution of the work. This must include the consultant's overseas staff, home-office staff, temporary employees in the host country, and possibly temporary staff, which may be expatriates, local professionals and technicians, or third-country nationals.

Direct-Expense Cost

The second cost is the direct-expense cost. This should cover transportation of personnel from the home office to the job site (and any other locations that may be involved), per diems while enroute, the housing and living expenses of staff and their families while away from home, rental of office space and living quarters as required, the acquisition of equipment and furniture, and finally, such extras as preparation of personnel to travel, including medical expenses, passports, visas, and time off to get ready to go and to return.

Overhead

Next comes overhead. There exists no established rule as to the application of overheads. Some companies operate only one accounting system, which includes domestic and international work, and, as such, they have only one overhead. Others have different corporate setups for work within the United States and overseas. These companies work with two different overheads, or more if they happen to be established in the host country, or elsewhere abroad where they maintain separate records, often under different accounting procedures. Overhead is frequently subject to much discussion during negotiating sessions, and participants should be well prepared with in-depth material, certified statements, etc., to prove their figures.

Subcontracts and Outside Services

Another item to consider is contracts and/or outside services, which should include a reasonable overhead markup, as these must be administered and controlled.

Local Costs

Difficult to calculate at the home office is the cost for translations, legal counsel, import duties, taxes, professional registration, drivers, guards, etc., as most of these are determined locally and must be arranged overseas. Sometimes the client is in the position to provide services and exemption from taxes and duties so that these items need not be estimated as items of cost. However, they are always present somewhere, and must not be overlooked in the contract preparation.

Escalation of Time and Expense Costs

International engagements often are long ones. Not only may an engineering project call for staged initial work, such as investment studies, feasibility studies, and preliminary design, before going into final design, specifications, and supervision of construction, but every one of these phases may be subject to lengthy examinations by the client. Also, the international financial institutions and development agencies, if interested or involved, require extensive reviews. Consultants should carefully take into account the possible increase of time, costs, and expenses from year to year, and include a protective covering provision in the contract language.

Contingency

Estimating costs and expenses, particularly for lump-sum contracts, is a risky matter even for the most experienced. I strongly recommend that a contingency factor be worked into the cost estimate so as to provide protection against variables that cannot be foreseen.

Profit

Finally, the consulting firm will have to establish a level of profit, and this, more often than not, is a percentage added to the total costs. There has been much debate over the years as to what this percentage should amount to. I know of no hard and fast rule that can be applied. Instead, I would recommend that, according to the complexity of the engagement, the profit be closely held within the same range as on similar engagements in the United States.

Special Conditions

The fourth and last of the special areas that must be looked into prior to contract negotiation is that of the special conditions. No two consulting engagements are alike and rarely, if ever, can two contracts be safely written with exactly the same language incorporating the same conditions. Special conditions apply particularly to circumstances that will influence the execution of the work and have an impact on the consultant's ability to perform and to control his costs. In some countries, an engineering consultant is required to register as a practicing professional. This is usually a costly and time-consuming procedure; if the contracting party is legally entitled to exempt its consultants from registration, this should be clearly stated in the agreement. Import restrictions can seriously delay the start-up of works and hinder normal working procedures of a firm that is accustomed to furnishing its personnel with modern instruments, equipment, and vehicles. Customs duties, levied by most governments on all imports, can require substantial outlays. Exemptions therefrom must be clearly stated under the special conditions. The same applies to corporate income taxes, personal income taxes of the consultant's personnel, and any other contributions that are not normally included under direct costs.

In a number of foreign countries, the cost of housing and transportation is extremely high. I know of several nations where, for example, housing simply will not be made available unless a one- or two-year contract is written and the full amount of the rental is paid in advance. Similarly, any vehicle imported may cost ten times more than its original price at the point of shipment. If the client recognizes these facts and agrees to provide housing and transportation services in order to keep the contract cost low, these points should be clearly enumerated. All these are applicable items of cost that must be incorporated into the fee estimate.

Then there is the rather basic matter of personnel and their interaction with the client. Essentially, most consultants are persons who perform professional services by dedicating their time to a project. Consultants are qualified because of education and experience. Some professionals are excellent team workers and adapt readily to different conditions. Others do not fit this pattern. Every once in a while differences of opinion and clashes of personality develop that require replacement of personnel. This is something that even occurs within the United States and causes some difficulty to management. But, when an employee and family are located halfway around the world, such replacement becomes a very serious and expensive matter. I normally prepare a clause to the effect that the consultant agrees to replace an employee at the client's request, but that the cost of the replacement shall be for the account of the client, unless the employee has not performed in accordance with his position requirements or has misbehaved on the job. Only then would the cost be borne by the consultant.

Other clauses that form part of the special conditions should detail the facilities that the client will provide the consultant. When dealing with sovereign governments, it is recommended to have a written confirmation in the agreement to the effect that any claims against the consultant in the performance of his duties will be handled and settled by the client's attorneys at no cost to the consultant.

PREPARING TO NEGOTIATE ABROAD

The following checklist shows some of the prime concerns that need to be confirmed by on-the-spot investigations:

Becoming Acquainted with the Local Scenario

1. Language Proficiency
2. Legal Considerations
3. Tax Implications
4. Professional Registration
5. Financial Profiles and Banking Facilities
6. Powers of Attorney to Negotiate Contracts and Sign Agreements

Subsequent to preparing the strategy for negotiations and reviewing in detail the proposed scope of work, the compensation, and the general and special conditions, the stage is now set for moving to the conference table. In years past it was not uncommon that a foreign client would travel to the consultant's home office and negotiate a contract there. It still occurs from time to time that agreements for work in certain countries are negotiated elsewhere, particularly when the international financial agencies and development institutions are involved. As a general rule, however, negotiations nowadays take place in the client's country and in his office, and this is good. If a consultant has not been in the client's country, I would strongly advise that he spend sufficient time there prior to the start-up of negotiations to acquaint himself with local conditions before sitting down at the negotiating table. Ignorance about ever-changing local conditions has caused too many misunderstandings and later disagreements, which easily could have been avoided by means of a timely visit.

Language Proficiency

One of the most important factors that must be recognized from the outset is that the knowledge of the client's language is absolutely indispensable in practically every case. Language capabilities are mentioned in other chapters of this book. As far as negotiations are concerned, it cannot be overemphasized that each and every word must be fully understood by the negotiating parties. Contracts are written in one or two languages nowadays. Usually, the host country's language is declared the ruling one, and this should be written into the agreement. It is a fact that, as many foreign clients speak English and unfortunately only few American professionals have ventured into foreign languages, negotiations are sometimes conducted in English. However, be that as it may, the ruling contract language of the formal agreement will be the binding one, and anybody preparing to negotiate a contract is well advised either to be sure to have a complete knowledge of the foreign language or to have available a capable and trustworthy translator-interpreter. American embassies and local chambers of commerce usually have a list of skilled translators.

Legal Considerations and Tax Implications

As important as the language itself is the need to have a full and comprehensive understanding of legal implications and tax considerations. What is perfectly normal and understood in this country under old, established Anglo-Saxon law is often totally different under the concepts of even older Roman law. Where the basic concepts of taxation have long become so complicated in the United States that there exist highly specialized tax accountants and lawyers, special circumstances and conditions in other countries have made taxes even more complicated and often totally confusing to outsiders. It is an absolute must for anybody starting up negotiations overseas to have first-class counsel available in matters of law and taxation. Again, the diplomatic representation of the United States of America, chambers of commerce, and local banks usually have lists of knowledgeable individuals and firms who are available.

Professional Registration

I mentioned before, when talking about special conditions, that some countries require the local professional registration of individuals and firms. Generally this is not insurmountable; but in some countries it can be very time consuming and there are a few where registration is quite expensive also. Professional registration should be carefully checked out prior to contract negotiations.

Financial Profiles and Banking Facilities

Finally, but not of least significance, I usually recommend establishing a contact with a reputable local bank to get a reading about local monetary conditions, convertibility of currency into foreign exchange, rates of interest, and other related financial matters. Bankers, whether they are independent locals or representatives of foreign banks, are usually reliable sources for information and guidance. I have avoided more than one pitfall by discussing the financial aspects of proposed forthcoming negotiations this way. However, as previously mentioned, bankers are not bound by their code of ethics to maintain the confidentiality of nonclient activities. Therefore it is necessary to be selective and discreet until a permanent relationship has been established.

Powers of Attorney

A power of attorney to negotiate and to sign on behalf of a firm in itself is a good example of the know-how and patience required for international work. The document first is drawn up by the company's attorneys and then signed by an executive officer and witnessed by the secretary before a notary public. Next, the notary public's signature and license is attested to by the county clerk, the county clerk's by the secretary of the state where the firm is incorporated, and the secretary of state's by the Secretary of State of the United States of America, whose office signs and affixes the American seal to the document.

Subsequently, procedures vary from country to country. Generally, a foreign consular official attests to the true signature of the U.S. Secretary of State, and the document is then valid. Sometimes, official translations of everything (including the language of stamps, signatures, and seals) have to be provided by a duly licensed official; and, in a few nations, the power of attorney must be deposited with government agencies overseas, registered, authenticated, and approved before it is valid and in force. The cost may vary from $10 to $200, excluding attorney's fees, but the time involved easily takes several weeks.

Getting Ready for the Negotiating Sessions

After all the above preparations, the time has finally come to sit face-to-face with the client and to start negotiating. Regardless of the location and circumstances, I have always tried to establish from the very beginning an atmosphere of mutual confidence and trust. In some countries where bargaining is an honored and lengthy business custom, I have made it my first point to let it be known that I have all the time in the world available that may be necessary for the negotiations. In other places, I have found it expedient to assert from the very beginning that I have come fully prepared with all my homework done and that I am ready to discuss details starting immediately.

Many years ago, in the Middle East, I once spent the first two full sessions discussing ancient cultures, national aspirations, and international politics. The specific contract negotiations that followed took only half the normal time but were successful. On the other hand, in a Northern European country where "time is money" even more so than in the United States, a proposed form of agreement prepared beforehand was presented to the clients at breakfast, discussed that morning, and signed immediately following lunch. Again, as in so many matters concerning international work, there are no hard and fast rules. The successful negotiator is well prepared and adapts himself to the customs and habits of his clients and thereby establishes his ability to work harmoniously in their country. Nothing is more detrimental than to advise a prospective client that you have only limited time available for negotiations. A professional consultant must be prepared to spend considerable time in the deliberations leading to a contract and I can not emphasize enough the importance that each and every point of the agreement be clearly understood by both sides before a contract is signed and sealed.

Compensation

When discussing compensation at the negotiating table, it is desirable to obtain an early decision as to the proposed mode of payment. In the past, American consultants were mostly paid in U.S. dollars, the Italians in lire, the Japanese in yen, etc. Nowadays, it is not that simple.

Because of international monetary market restrictions and foreign exchange fluctuations, the majority of foreign clients propose to pay a portion of the consultant's compensation in local currency and a part in foreign exchange, not necessarily in the currency of the consultant's country. When the international financial institutions and development agencies are involved, local (onshore) expenses are usually covered by the borrower (the host country) in local currency as part of their contribution to the project, and the foreign (offshore) expenditures are paid by the lender in the consultant's currency. It behooves the negotiator to investigate this matter carefully so that he will not get entangled in any undue currency problems and exchange risks. As a rule of thumb, international consultants today try to cover their expatriates' salaries, overhead, and profit in guaranteed hard currency foreign exchange, and to accept local currency for local costs and onshore expenses.

The need to separate local costs from foreign costs complicates the payment portion of the compensation clauses, but once laid out in detail, no further difficulties should be encountered in this respect.

The other factor determining compensation is the form of payment, requiring thought from the outset. Any client should be checked out in advance as to his financial capability and general standing in his and the international community. This, unfortunately, is easier said than done. Many banks and the U.S. Department of Commerce can provide information on individuals and industries. But who will venture to offer experienced advice with regard to, say, a new government in a small, lesser-developed nation? It will be up to the consultant to avail himself of the best possible sources of information and then to use judgment. Thanks to the Export-Import Bank of the United States and the Foreign Credit Insurance Association (FCIA), some commercial and political risks for the service industry are now insurable, and if a U.S. consulting firm proposes to enter into an agreement overseas, it may be well advised to avail itself of the above-mentioned insurance facilities which are available at a reasonable cost. The Overseas Private Investment Corporation (OPIC), another U.S. government-sponsored entity primarily active in the foreign investment sector, also offers insurance programs. (OPIC should not be confused with OPEC, the Organization of Petroleum Exporting Countries.)

Establishing Conditions of Payment

There are many established procedures for payment of services. Only in a few countries (unfortunately very few today) are a simple written agreement and a handshake more valid than the most complicated documented conditions of payment. Sometimes, notes issued by the client and predated in accordance with the terms of the contract can be obtained and are acceptable, as they can be discounted by the banks and thereby serve as working capital for the consultant. Clients in general are not averse to paying mobilization expenses and progress payments. The difficulty is, sometimes, how to assure that these payments will come through within a reasonable time. Experience has shown, for instance, that frequently a client authorizes payment, but the banking and government bureaucracy delays the transfer of funds. Thus while the client has paid, the consultant does not receive his money. There is no universal remedy for this situation. However, there are a few measures that can be observed and should be incorporated, where possible, into the compensation clauses.

Revolving Funds and Letters of Credit

Whenever local funds are concerned, a procedure can be followed whereby these funds are deposited by the client into a bank account ahead of the consultant's billing, so that when the final invoice comes through, the money is readily available. This can be done through the creation of a revolving fund or the establishment of a letter of credit in local funds. As far as payment in foreign exchange is concerned, the best and safest way is to obtain an irrevocable and confirmed letter of credit that permits the consulting firm to draw against the client's funds as soon as billings have been properly authorized by the client. Incidentally, it is important that letters of credit in foreign exchange be irrevocable (i.e., that they cannot be canceled out before the date of expiration) and confirmed effect (i.e., that the foreign exchange has actually been deposited overseas into the account of the bank that handles the transaction). The only possible shortcoming of an irrevocable and confirmed letter of credit is that, under normal conditions, a consulting firm needs to have its billings certified by the client before it can proceed to collect. Lately, a technique has been developed that permits a firm to collect, say, thirty days after invoices have been presented to the client, unless the client protests the billings. This procedure has alleviated some of the hardships that come about through bureaucratic delays and is recommended to be included in the payment clause.

U.S. Dollars Versus Foreign Currencies

American consultants have traditionally been reluctant to receive payments in currency other than U.S. dollars. Competitive situations have, little by little, forced the acceptability of payment in local currency. I believe it will not be long now before the U.S. international consultant will be ready to accept French francs, German marks, Mexican pesos, etc. Discussing this matter at one of the American Consulting Engineers Council's recent international workshops, we were amused by the story of one of the principals of a large firm who had reluctantly agreed to accept a substantial payment for services in a Middle Eastern currency, only to find that at the time of collection the U.S. dollar had declined in value and he was reaping an unexpected bonanza substantially above the anticipated profit for the job. Alas, there are many cases where this kind of situation did not have such a fortunate ending. Therefore, the matter of payments requires expert attention at the negotiating table.

THE ART OF NEGOTIATING

Professionals, except for lawyers, are not normally the world's best negotiators. Consultants know it and, as I am finding out more and more, our clients know it too. Negotiating a consulting contract is an art which requires the skillful give-and-take that makes for a final harmonious agreement between a client and his future consultant. Negotiating incorporates an element of bargaining that is alien to many of us in the professions. Nevertheless, negotiating is a vital part of the practice of consulting and must be performed in an efficient and ethical manner.

For many contracts, large established international consulting firms send out not just one individual but a negotiating team, which may include the writer of the original proposal, an accountant or financial expert, the proposed project manager, and an attorney in addition to a corporate officer.

Others not as yet experienced in protracted sessions overseas should seriously consider engaging a negotiator for the purpose of enjoying the best possible advice and guidance. There are specialists available for such short-time assignments, particularly older, semiretired consultants who have spent a lifetime in the international arena.

The first meeting across the conference table is frequently the most difficult one. Client and consultant maneuver for position. Proposal language is brought out of dusty file cabinets. "These are our standard conditions of contract," say the people sitting opposite to you. "We have just concluded agreements with your competitors from another country with none of the special conditions you are proposing," states somebody else. "Look at these costs. There is no special provision for vacation pay or educational expenses." That is the time to quietly take notes, patiently explore details, make comparisons, and firmly search for inconsistencies and unsubstantiated claims. This careful work will lead to mutually satisfactory solutions. While the final contract price is important to the parties, the deciding factor at all times should remain the high quality of the services to be performed. Neither the original request for a proposal (RFP) nor the actual proposal submitted should be ignored, but exploratory probing of the full scope of services, the interplay of general and special conditions, as well as compensation and payment, will soon clear the atmosphere and set the stage for the final conclusive bargaining.

I do not recommend that design consultants enter into fee discussions with inflated costs and unreasonable fee demands. Rather, a first contract proposal may well include some fringes and extras that a client with a limited budget can eliminate. It is comforting to know that a comparison of U.S. practices and costs versus those of other industrial nations will establish that American design professionals have been competitive in the international marketplace since the devaluation of the U.S. dollar a few years ago.

Negotiating ideally takes place in a calm and friendly atmosphere. It may be quite natural for one or the other individual to become excited; but certainly, discussions should be conducted tactfully and with mutual respect and consideration. Irritating differences in international negotiations are sometimes caused by language difficulties, and these should be resolved immediately. If certain "roadblocks" cannot be overcome in one session, push them back for a day or two, when they might be resolved in a different atmosphere. My experience is that a hard but serious negotiation session establishes a bond of mutual respect between the consultant and his client. This is the case domestically just as it is in the international marketplace. The only real difference is that overseas, a negotiator must be an expert in his field of professional endeavor in addition to being a combination statesman, diplomat, and solid citizen.

FINISHING UP SUCCESSFUL NEGOTIATIONS

One last word about negotiating abroad. Nowhere is an agreement binding until a contract has been signed. Overseas, a document has to be drawn up and may have to pass inspection in two languages, official ratification by various government agencies, and approval by third parties, such as the international financing agencies. Foreign signatories usually need written, authorized powers of attorney.

When dealing with sovereign governments, an official opinion of the attorney general as to the legality of the proceedings and documentation may be necessary; and, after that, perhaps confirmation by the board of exchange or central bank.

Invariably, once the negotiator departs, the processing of contract documents has a tendency to slow down and to suffer from totally unexpected difficulties. Therefore, a negotiation should be firmly concluded as soon as possible. A few extra days with the client will be well worth the time and save delay, anguish, and expense later on.

Personally, I enjoy international negotiations. They present a challenge second to none. I have been fortunate enough to develop real friendships with some of my clients because of tough negotiating sessions with much bargaining that developed mutual respect. The basic ingredients for a successful negotiation, wherever it may be, are preparation, flexibility, forthrightness, and, above all, honesty.

STAFFING FOR MULTINATIONAL ENGAGEMENTS

Staffing multinational engagements is a most challenging task for the management of any consulting firm. Of basic concern for every international organization is to have reliable people available and willing to go overseas as openings present themselves. Therefore, general personnel policies should include the international aspects of a consulting practice so as to have a pool of talent upon which to draw. Particularly delicate is the selection of a person to go overseas for a specific assignment, be it short- or long-term. If care has been taken with proper recruitment procedures, such a candidate can be found from within the company. Oftentimes, however, firms must go into the employment market and search for somebody with the necessary qualifications and experience.

MANAGEMENT

Let us take a first look at management. An experienced international executive who has had top-level responsibilities overseas will have relatively few difficulties assuming a similar or superior domestic position. It is quite significant that many corporate top executives of large firms have served in varying positions abroad at one time or another. On the other hand, a manager with high-level responsibilities and an excellent domestic record may quickly run into problems and difficulties in the international arena—which can be disastrous to everyone concerned. Therefore, when staffing for a multinational engagement, the basic premise is to have at least one permanent member on the firm's management team who is not only interested but also experienced in international work. As a company spreads out its activities into different parts of the world, top-level management must be available for the execution of multinational operations. In another part of this book, we will examine the role of the various levels of management in the performance of international work. This particular chapter is dedicated to the internal management tasks of staffing, and we shall take it for granted that among the principals of a firm there is at least one executive with sound overseas experience and a proven record of successful management.

RECRUITING

As a general recommendation, consulting firms that desire to perform professional services outside their country should follow a policy of recruiting personnel in all categories who are interested in multinational work. Naturally, this is easier said than done. Nevertheless, it is sound management philosophy to give preference to applicants who have worked overseas or who are interested in international developments if there is reason to believe that the company may want to involve its members in international work at one time or another. When there are direct job openings or vacancies for engagements in specific countries, then, of course, it is quite obvious that only a candidate who is fully responsive to the professional requirements of the position should be selected.

First-class professionals willing to travel and/or transfer overseas are hard to come by. Increasingly, consulting firms look to personnel specialists to search for, interview, and engage overseas members. Frequently, as the time available to fill a vacancy is short, extensive advertising and interviewing may be necessary. A newcomer to this field may be surprised at the number of responses to a recruiting advertisement for overseas work. It will not be long, however, before it becomes obvious that there exist a good many people who roam the world and hop from job to job. Many of these may have performed well at one time or another, but quite a few eventually develop into a type of international adventurer whose services will benefit neither employer nor client. Résumés should be carefully read, references painstakingly checked, degrees and registrations verified, and personal interviews held with the candidate and at times also with the candidate's spouse and family.

The need to get to know as much as possible about the personality, philosophy, and family of a prospective overseas employee cannot be sufficiently stressed. Regardless of the technical competence, string of degrees, or impressive social background, strongly prejudiced persons, eternally pessimistic worriers, and prima donnas generally do not work out. These characteristics may become magnified once the individual is removed from the home office and has to perform away from the restraints of customary environment and surroundings. Among the international job hoppers, there are quite a few who are superbly qualified as professionals, but who have become used to "the good life" in foreign countries with high pay, no taxes, domestic servants, commissary rights, and even diplomatic privileges. Some of the work of the past few decades in the less-developed countries has lead simple, solid citizens to suddenly regard themselves as entitled to varieties of privileges. Beware of these!

Many firms now make it a practice to interview the candidate's spouse as thoroughly as the candidate. There is good reason for this. A dissatisfied, uncooperative partner can easily become an insurmountable liability and bring about the candidate's complete failure on the job overseas. When there are teenaged children in the family, it is not out of order to take a look at them. Some youngsters these days have developed customs and habits which are not acceptable in certain sovereign nations. I will leave it to the reader to conclude what could happen if a 14-year-old is unwilling to submit to parental discipline and misbehaves in a foreign country.

Most firms have a policy of preferentially staffing overseas jobs with personnel who have been with the company for some time. This, I believe, is wise in every respect. Yet international management should not take the employee's past domestic record as complete assurance of similar performance abroad. Even here, it is recommended that a careful personal interview be conducted, including the employee's family.

International engagements require personnel ranging from highly specialized, experienced professionals to skilled technicians to capable administrators. Position descriptions should be in writing, detailing each opening and defining the authority, responsibilities, and functions, as well as the organizational relationship and performance objectives. Often it will not be possible to locate the ideal candidate, so that compromises will have to be made. In this connection, it may be well to remember that requirements to perform adequately in one country often differ from those in another. For instance, professional registration is a determinant for employment of an architect or an engineer in the United States, whereas the ability to speak the language of the host country may be of greater importance for the successful performance of a job in Arabia or in French-speaking Africa. Technical proficiency in air conditioning will be of little consequence 10,000 feet above sea level in the South American Andes. Experience with cost-saving devices need not be considered important in labor-intensive markets. Hence, careful attention should be focused on the different values and their priorities.

Most consultants, because of the nature of their work, are required to travel extensively. A well-organized firm performing services away from its home office normally establishes procedures and policies covering business travel. Companies with engagements in more than one state and possibly a number of branch offices will have guidelines for their members when away from home. International staffing demands more than this. It requires expert management—initially to hire and assign the best-qualified and available employees for overseas work, then to properly prepare them for the engagement, and finally to give them continued and encouraging support at all times. The successful execution of a foreign engagement depends as much upon the professional expertise of the firm and its members as on its internal organization, administrative competence, and personnel relations.

EMPLOYMENT MANUALS

When staffing for multinational engagements, it is recommended that established patterns be followed that have been perfected over the years. In order to avoid misunderstandings, which arise so easily over long distances, international consultants should issue printed policy and procedure manuals to serve management as well as employees. A typical company policy statement covering housing and furniture is provided on pages 97 and 100–102 of this chapter.

From time to time, as a matter of fact, company policy memoranda may also have to be presented to clients during negotiations and audits in order to establish and justify costs. Detailed, written manuals, therefore, are of particular importance for the orderly conduct of all matters concerning recruiting, employment, personnel relations, and control of costs, as well as client understanding.

EMPLOYMENT CONTRACTS

For domestic employment, consulting firms rarely enter into formal contractual agreements with their employees. However, the staffing for international work requires that companies develop basic employment conditions and write clearly defined employment contracts when sending full-time international staff out of the domestic scene into foreign lands. Ideally, the contract should specify that the employee accepts an overseas position for a determined time or an assignment abroad for its duration. As a minimum, the contract should be so worded that it gives the firm the representation required to handle its objectives overseas and cover the consultant's obligations to the client with regard to staffing for the work to be performed.

When a company incorporates overseas, maintains foreign task forces or branch offices, and customarily transfers members from its domestic offices to international posts and vice versa, the terms of employment contracts will have to be legally binding and should be compatible with the governing laws of the host country where the employee will be stationed. In many parts of the world, there exist substantial differences in legal coverage of social security, forms of insurance and basic compensation, tax retention, etc. An overseas employee contract should incorporate general provisions that define the responsibilities of the employee and the company vis-à-vis all such obligations. It is also useful to have an international employment contract stipulate the procedures to be followed in case of disagreements and termination. Finally, it is recommended that, whenever possible, the laws of the employer's country of incorporation apply. This will avoid the situation in which a firm finds itself served with papers in a foreign country by an employee who might have been persuaded that legal action somewhere overseas provides him a better chance to win his case. At the same time, of course, most employees recognize the advantage and usually prefer to be fully covered under the laws of a country with which they are generally familiar.

Employment contracts not only provide security for employer and employee alike, but are also valuable documents supporting client relationships, in particular when a consulting firm has agreed to perform certain works with specific personnel and when, through no fault of the firm, the designated full-time international member suddenly is no longer available and this needs to be substantiated to a client.

For short-term trips abroad and temporary duty overseas, employment contracts are not necessary, but even here a brief matter-of-fact letter of understanding can be helpful.

CLASSIFICATION OF INTERNATIONAL STAFF

Now let us take a close look at the most important areas that require clear understanding by a firm and its international staff members. First, there are generally accepted basic definitions in the consulting world which categorize four different classifications of international employees.

1. *Full-Time International Staff (FIS)* An FIS is a resident of the country where his firm is established and is stationed overseas with his family for extended periods. Full-time international staff are normally recruited specifically for international assignments or are transferred on a long-term basis from domestic operations.
2. *Temporary International Staff (TIS)* A TIS is a resident of the country where his firm is established and is stationed overseas on temporary duty. Temporary international staff may be transferred from domestic operations for periods normally not exceeding 90 days or may be recruited especially for some particular short-term job.
3. *Third-Country Staff (TCS)* A TCS is a citizen of a country other than where the firm is established and where he is employed to perform his duties. Third-country staff may be stationed overseas with their families for extended periods or be charged, like a TIS, with temporary, short-term assignments.
4. *Host-Country Staff (HCS)* An HCS is a citizen of the country where an international engagement is being performed. He is usually engaged locally and resides permanently in the host country with his family.

The following are the principal areas that should be covered by company policy for multinational staffing:

STAFF COMPENSATION

Salary and Bonus

Base salary, incentive or management bonus, or any other form of compensation for FIS, TIS, and TCS categories should be in line with the firm's general domestic schedules so that employees transferring back from a foreign post do not find themselves faced with a cutback in basic pay. Below I describe the various ways to provide for adequate "international" compensation.

HCS members are generally placed on a company payroll commensurate with their qualifications and the going local rate of services that they are required to perform.

Length of Tour

Short-term and temporary overseas assignments do not call for extra compensation unless special circumstances exist, such as travel into dangerous areas, particularly severe climates, personal hardship, etc. A reasonable percentage added to the base salary can adequately take care of such cases.

When a TIS is required to travel abroad without interruption for a longer period than the maximum ninety days for short-term, then the employer may consider permitting the employee's family to join him. Alternatively, time may be added to normal domestic vacations or an incentive-management bonus may be considered upon the member's successful completion of his assignment and return to his home base.

FISs and TCSs are stationed overseas for a definite period, and normally return to their home base thereafter for domestic or foreign reassignment. However, reassignment should be made only after a reasonable period of rest and recreation.

HCSs' terms of employment should be similar to the domestic policies of a consultant, but must not conflict with customary practices in the host country. In case of conflict, host-country norms take precedence.

Overseas Differential (OSD)

Essentially, the OSD has been established to provide a cash incentive for an international assignment which separates and FIC and sometimes a TCS from his normal environment for an extended period. The OSD is computed as a percentage of base salary, and its magnitude depends upon the situation prevailing at the post as it affects living and working conditions. The overseas differential is a generally accepted part of an employee's compensation package making it attractive for an employee to transfer overseas.

Overseas Post Allowance (OPA)

Closely related to the overseas differential but still quite different is the overseas post allowance. The purpose of the OPA is to compensate employees for the relative difference of living costs between an assigned location and those in the country of their normal residence. Different formulas have been developed by the consulting industry and others. In the United States, more and more firms are following State Department formulas that were devised for the U.S. Foreign Service. U.S. government policies that not too long ago hardly competed with private industry have now become quite generous. Many firms prefer to adopt the State Department's guidelines and regulations instead of going to the trouble of developing their own.

Tax Equalization (TE)

Tax equalization is a complicated matter that requires considerable attention. Years ago, consultants were mostly exempt from income taxes overseas and other local surcharges (except for import duties, which have always been a factor to be considered). As foreign nations have come to establish income tax systems of their own, it is only reasonable to expect that foreigners should be taxed for salaries earned in the performance of work in that country. However, in a number of the developing countries, incomes stand at levels substantially below those of the industrialized nations and, therefore, a consulting professional who is in the, say, 30 to 40 percent tax bracket in the United States will suddenly find himself in a much higher tax bracket in the country where he is assigned. Clearly, a responsible employer must see to it that the payment of these taxes does not represent a financial hardship or penalty. Not only would it be practically impossible to hire and keep employees in certain countries, but the absence of a tax equalization policy would encourage tax cheating, which any self-respecting individual or firm must neither consider nor tolerate. The basic policy for tax equalization is to assure net compensation regardless of the country in which an employee is assigned.

Once in a while, consulting firms obtain contracts that provide for tax exemption, and there exist a few nations where income taxes in certain brackets lie below those of the United States. For these, the same tax equalization policy should apply and in turn the firm will benefit. I have known of concentrated new business efforts in certain "low tax" countries by consultants who are anxious to find for themselves a tax equalization bonus from lower taxes to compensate for the higher tax costs that they are absorbing from operations elsewhere.

HCSs are subject to taxation by their respective countries, and international consultants need not provide any special tax equalization. However, firms operating with HCSs should be careful to follow local laws and regulations as to tax withholding, collecting social security payments, and providing for severance pay reserves, Christmas and other holiday funds, etc.

Vacations and Home Leave

Company policy governing vacations forms part of the employment package. Vacations for overseas personnel are of exceptional importance inasmuch as the concern is not only to provide for a well-deserved time off from the daily work routine, but in many cases, a period of rest and recreation. This is absolutely essential, particularly when personnel are located in faraway places under difficult climatic conditions, for example. Also, for those working in an isolated post, morale is boosted by planning and looking forward to official periods of vacation.

Generally, vacation policy for full-time international staff located overseas is divided into two categories. First, there are local vacations. These are usually one to two weeks taken overseas with the employer providing the time and the employee paying the cost of the transportation and accommodations wherever he may choose to go. Second, there are home leaves or terminal vacations, for which the company assumes the full expenses of time and travel. I have found that many U.S. consultants allow a minimum of one month of home leave for each year of overseas residence.

In addition to local vacations and home leave, well-organized companies also specify holidays which include customary U.S. holidays and which the firm's employees are entitled to observe regardless of where they may be residing; for example, the First of January (New Year's Day), the Fourth of July (Independence Day), and the Twenty-fifth of December (Christmas Day). These holidays should be authorized in addition to the customary holidays of the host country. A clear-cut vacation and holiday policy not only is helpful as a matter of procedure, but also serves to calculate yearly working hours and the cost of man-hours when estimating jobs and negotiating contracts.

TISs require no different vacation policy from the customary domestic one, except for special considerations as mentioned above.

HCSs' vacations should follow the established industry pattern of the host country and are frequently prescribed in local labor laws.

SICK LEAVE

A very important matter to most employees is the knowledge that in case of absence from regular duties during personal illness or serious sickness or death in the immediate family, there is a provision for reasonable company and insurance coverage. While most of the employment conditions and fringe benefits should equally apply to everyone, sick leave overseas is a concern which may lend itself to special consideration for particular cases. Professionals who have elderly parents, for instance, may be reluctant to accept an overseas assignment unless they are certain they will be permitted by the company to return home in case of need. A person with a large family may look for assurance that in case of sickness overseas, the family may, if necessary, return to "civilization" if they happen to be located in the wilderness. In my opinion, overseas sick leave policy should be kept flexible so as to accommodate different needs and different circumstances. A no-nonsense, yet reasonable sick leave policy will greatly contribute toward satisfied and effective overseas personnel performance.

MEDICAL EXAMINATIONS AND INSURANCE

Many employers nowadays require employees to take medical examinations prior to employment and enrollment in the company's health and life insurance plans. When international assignments are involved, medical examinations become particularly important. The simple cost of transportation to and from a job site half-way around the world in case of illness, not to speak of the loss of time, can seriously interfere with scheduling completion time of important works, and make the difference between profit and loss on a job. Exposure to new climatic conditions, different foods, and a variety of secondary circumstances can readily precipitate rapid changes in the conditions of health which, without a trip overseas, might not have become apparent for some time. Further, there are still many cases in the world where diseases are not yet under control, and where many illnesses are prevalent. Whoever becomes assigned to international staff, therefore, should have a thorough initial examination and periodic checkups. This applies equally to the employee's spouse and dependents.

Firms that maintain domestic group insurance policies covering the health and life of employees and their dependents should be careful to ensure that the protection extends to international travel as well as to worldwide medical treatment and hospitalization.

From time to time, when staffing key personnel for a particularly difficult and selective assignment, companies should take out special risk insurance policies on these employees. This is an extraordinary and certainly not a customary practice, but is well advised for exceptional cases.

Medical examinations and insurance are of particular significance in the FIS, TIS, and TCS categories. A number of foreign nations with advanced social legislation have requirements covering their nationals under varying degrees of health care and life insurance. HCSs should be provided by their foreign employer with reasonable benefits in this area so that there prevail no substantial differences between the various employee categories.

HOUSING AND FURNITURE

No uniform industry policy exists as to the provision of housing and furniture for members and their families stationed overseas. Some firms follow the well-publicized policies of the U.S. Department of State, others have issued their own housing allowances, and a few improvise according to circumstance.

International staff should be in the position to live in conditions reasonably equivalent to those at home. In some cases, the post allowance (see above) will permit the necessary adjustments. In others, the company may have to intervene directly and provide facilities. For such a case, it is advisable to specify what furniture and appliances the employer provides. This will permit employees to know in advance what to expect, so that suitable arrangements can be made.

A family temporarily residing overseas on an international assignment should be in the position to establish itself comfortably and securely in its new environment. However, luxury items, family heirlooms, and costly furnishings best are left at home or stored.

For the top management of an international task force, different policies may apply in regard to housing and furniture. A senior company representative may have as an important part of his job assignment the duty of entertaining and representing the company locally. Similarly, a single professional going abroad will have a different housing and furniture policy than one who transfers with a family.

The administration of housing and furniture policies is not easy and requires tact and skill. For some large engagements overseas, I would recommend that the consulting firm send ahead of the employees a knowledgeable member or two of the personnel or administrative departments in order to prepare for housing and to provide the basic necessary local living conditions. This may save both time and money in the long run, as it can facilitate recruiting overseas staff and also provide for initial contacts with local associates.

Detailed policies covering shipment of personal belongings, household goods, and furnishings, with limits as to weights or expense, are helpful in maintaining management control and in keeping up harmonious employee relationships. Once again, I might recommend the U.S. State Department's regulations in this area. They are well laid out and can be used with few if any changes.

EDUCATIONAL ALLOWANCE

The purpose of educational allowances is to assist the full-time international staff (FIS) located overseas in meeting educational costs incurred while abroad, which may be substantially higher than those incurred in their home community. Normally, overseas educational allowances are provided to pay for primary and secondary school education (kindergarten through twelfth grade) but not for college or university studies.

Allowances are sometimes authorized for foreign language lessons for employees and their spouses at the beginning of an international assignment. In addition, consulting firms generally permit dependent children of full-time international staff not residing with their parents abroad to travel and visit once a year during vacation time at company expense.

There exists no standard policy as to the application of educational allowances, travel expenses, etc. While the U.S. Department of State's policy in this connection is clearly defined, professional consultants in private practice may learn that they are unable to function under a government policy. Additional costs that may be incurred by the private sector will have to be incorporated in the direct cost of a particular engagement or as overhead for foreign operations.

Overseas clients sometimes object to what they regard as extravagances of the American educational system, and company policy for overseas educational allowances should be realistic as well as equitable. This of course applies not only to educational allowances, but also to many of the other items discussed above. A consulting firm must remain competitive in the international marketplace. After the initial development of staffing and employment policies, periodic reviews will be necessary.

A U.S. Department of State's table detailing salaries of government service (GS ratings) and the three grades of foreign service (FSO, FSR, FSS) effective October 12, 1975, is reproduced on pages 98 and 99. Consultants may find it helpful to be able to refer occasionally to current U.S. government compensation when establishing company salary rates and schedules.

Memo No. 005.374-R2 March 1, 1975

HOUSING AND FURNITURE

International

1. *Scope:* This memorandum states the company policy concerning housing and furniture for members posted overseas.

2. *Purpose:* The purpose of this memo is to standardize and facilitate the provision of housing and furniture for members stationed overseas and to provide a means for normalizing costs of housing and furniture.

3. *Applicability:* This memo applies to overseas members and third national members as defined in Memo No. 005.070. It does not apply to assigned members or local members as defined in Memo No. 005.070.

   Assigned members arrange for accommodations on a temporary basis and are reimbursed by expense account.

   No provisions are made for housing or furniture for local members.

4. *Basic Policy:* Preferably, members make arrangements for their own housing and furniture, subject to the approval of the Branch, Task Force, or Regional Manager. A *Housing Allowance,* as outlined below, is established at those posts where this practice is considered practicable by the company. The amount of the allowance is based upon the company's estimate of reasonable cost for housing and furniture, less the cost of similar facilities in Chicago called the "home equivalent."

   At posts where the use of housing allowance is not practicable in the judgment of the company, housing and furniture is provided in kind by the company, as outlined under *Alternate Policy.* The member reimburses the company on the basis of reasonable cost of furnishing the facilities in Chicago designated herein as the "home equivalent."

DEPARTMENT OF STATE SALARY TABLES

Rates Effective October 12, 1975, Established by Executive Order No. 11883

Executive Salaries

Secretary of State	$63,000
Deputy Secretary and Chiefs of Class 1 Missions	$44,600
Under Secretaries and Chiefs of Class 2 Missions	$42,000
Deputy Under Secretary, Assistant Secretaries, others of Assistant Secretary rank, Career Ambassadors, and Chiefs of Class 3 Missions	$39,900
Career Ministers and Chiefs of Class 4 Missions	$37,800

General Schedule and Foreign Service Salaries

CATEGORY AND GRADE				STEP RATES WITHIN GRADE LEVEL OR CLASS (Dollars)									
GS	FSO	FSR	FSS	1	2	3	4	5	6	7	8	9	10
18				37,800*									
	1	1		37,800*	37,800*	37,800*							
17				37,800*	37,800*	37,800*	37,800*	37,800*					
16				36,338	37,549	37,800*	37,800*	37,800*	37,800*	37,800*	37,800*	37,800*	
	2	2		36,092	37,295	37,800*	37,800*	37,800*	37,800*	37,800*			
15				31,309	32,353	33,397	34,441	35,485	36,529	37,573	37,800*	37,800*	37,800
	3	3		28,582	29,535	30,488	31,441	32,394	33,347	34,300			
			1	28,582	29,535	30,488	31,441	32,394	33,347	34,300	35,253	36,206	37,159
14				26,861	27,756	28,651	29,546	30,441	31,336	32,231	33,126	34,021	34,916
	4	4		22,906	23,670	24,434	25,198	25,962	26,726	27,490			
13			2	22,906	23,670	24,434	25,198	25,962	26,726	27,490	28,254	29,018	29,782

12			19,386	20,032	20,678	21,324	21,970	22,616	23,262	23,908	24,554	25,200
	5		18,612	19,232	19,852	20,472	21,092	21,712	22,332			
		3	18,612	19,232	19,852	20,472	21,092	21,712	22,332	22,952	23,572	24,192
11			16,255	16,797	17,339	17,881	18,423	18,965	19,507	20,049	20,591	21,133
	6		15,359	15,871	16,383	16,895	17,407	17,919	18,431			
		4	15,359	15,871	16,383	16,895	17,407	17,919	18,431	18,943	19,455	19,967
10			14,824	15,318	15,812	16,306	16,800	17,294	17,788	18,282	18,776	19,270
		5	13,770	14,229	14,688	15,147	15,606	16,065	16,524	16,983	17,442	17,901
9			13,482	13,931	14,380	14,829	15,278	15,727	16,176	16,625	17,074	17,523
	7		12,899	13,329	13,759	14,189	14,619	15,049	15,479			
		6	12,345	12,757	13,169	13,581	13,993	14,405	14,817	15,229	15,641	16,053
8			12,222	12,629	13,036	13,443	13,850	14,257	14,664	15,071	15,478	15,885
		7	11,068	11,437	11,806	12,175	12,544	12,913	13,282	13,651	14,020	14,389
	8		11,046	11,414	11,782	12,150	12,518	12,886	13,254			
7			11,046	11,414	11,782	12,150	12,518	12,886	13,254	13,622	13,990	14,358
6			9,946	10,278	10,610	10,942	11,274	11,606	11,938	12,270	12,602	12,934
		8	9,923	10,254	10,585	10,916	11,247	11,578	11,909	12,240	12,571	12,902
5			8,925	9,223	9,521	9,819	10,117	10,415	10,713	11,011	11,309	11,607
		9	8,896	9,193	9,490	9,787	10,084	10,381	10,678	10,975	11,272	11,569
4		10	7,976	8,242	8,508	8,774	9,040	9,306	9,572	9,838	10,104	10,370
3			7,102	7,339	7,576	7,813	8,050	8,287	8,524	8,761	8,998	9,235
2			6,296	6,506	6,716	6,926	7,136	7,346	7,556	7,766	7,976	8,186
1			5,559	5,744	5,929	6,114	6,299	6,484	6,669	6,854	7,039	7,224

* Salary for employees at these rates is limited by Section 5308, Title 5 of the U.S. Code to the rate for Level V of the Executive Schedule.

5. *Housing Allowance:* Housing allowances are established for designated posts by the International Division Head upon recommendation of the Regional Manager in concurrence with Corporate Administration. Allowances are computed on a monthly basis, including:

    a. Approximate rental for a residence of acceptable quality and condition, providing accommodations as set forth below in Paragraph 8.

    b. The approximate purchase cost of "hard" furniture meeting the standards listed in Paragraph 8 amortized over a 60-month period.

    c. 2% of estimated amounts for furniture to cover maintenance and insurance.

    d. Less an amount equal to the "home equivalent" as provided for in Paragraph 7.

    e. Members providing their own housing and furniture are responsible for such lease agreement as may be required and to the lessor for proper utilization and maintenance of the property rented to them.

6. *Alternate Policy:* At posts or on assignments where the use of housing allowance is not practicable in the judgment of the company, housing and furniture is provided in kind by the company and the member pays the company rental on the basis of the "home equivalent" as determined below.

    When housing and furniture are supplied by the company, the provisions of Paragraphs 8 and 9 apply.

7. *Home Equivalent:* Home equivalent of cost of housing and furniture is computed at 10% of base salary. Home equivalent is normally deducted as of the date the member arrives at the assigned post except in cases approved prior to departure, when the member must temporarily maintain two households for family convenience. Home equivalent continues until reassignment to a new post, termination, or such other reason that the member is no longer considered assigned to the post. Home equivalent continues during vacations taken while assigned to the post and during end of tour vacations so long as the member is to return to the post for subsequent assignment.

8. *Facilities Provided:* The company will normally provide housing, furniture, and appliances in accordance with the following:

a. A member on single status or with wife only: living and dining area, one or two bedrooms, kitchen, and bath. Furniture as listed in Appendix A.

b. Member with wife and children: living and dining area, kitchen, bath, one master bedroom plus additional bedrooms with the approval of the International Division Head. Furniture as listed in Appendix A.

9. *Responsibility:* Members are responsible for the safekeeping, maintenance, and proper use of housing, yards, gardens, other related buildings, and furniture and appliances assigned to them. Members meet the cost of all utilities. At the conclusion of occupancy, such facilities are to be returned in the same condition as received, subject only to normal wear and tear.

   Members are liable for damage to facilities and property caused by negligent or improper use and care.

10. *Effectivity:* This memo is effective as of March 1, 1975.

11. *Supersedes:* This memo supersedes Memo No. 005.374-R1 dated June 22, 1972.

   Issued by:

   ____

Attachment to Memo No. 005.374-R2

Company-provided Furniture and Appliances

Kitchen	Range, electric, gas, or kerosene Refrigerator-freezer Water filter (if required) Water heater Work table (if required) Cupboard (if required)
Laundry	Washing machine
Dining Room	Table Buffet or dish cupboard Six chairs
Living Room	Settee Two lounge chairs Coffee table

Two end tables
Two lamps
Table for record player
Ventilating fan of appropriate size and type

Bedrooms	Double or twin beds in master bedroom One twin bed per child One chest drawers per family member One night table per bed, two per double bed One lamp per night table One straight chair per family member One vanity top and mirror per bedroom Air conditioner per bedroom if climate dictates, with approval of International Division Head Space heaters, if climate dictates, with approval of International Division Head Provision for hanging clothes, if not built-in closets

FINANCING AN INTERNATIONAL OPERATION

Working capital has to be readily available for every orderly ongoing enterprise. Particularly at times when money is difficult to raise even at high rates of interest, appropriate financing needs expert attention. In the international arena, consultants must take into account a number of special factors.

MOBILIZATION

The cost of starting up an overseas engagement can be very substantial, as funds may be needed for some or all the following:

Preparation of Personnel:	Physicals, shots, medical certificates for employees and dependents Passports, visas and special permits for employees and dependents Storage of household goods; export boxing and moving of personal belongings and household goods Rental of overseas housing Prepayment of tuition for employees and dependents
Purchases:	Office supplies Office and field equipment Automobiles and trucks

Transportation:	Travel for employees and dependents Per diems for employees and dependents Baggage charges for employees and dependents Shipping charges and insurance premiums for office supplies, office and field equipment, automobiles, trucks, personal belongings, and household goods
Miscellaneous:	Special insurance: Accident and health; life; special hazards—fire, earthquake, floods Rental of office space Retainers for representatives, agents, lawyers Import duties, tax stamps, or bonds in lieu thereof Initial deposits into foreign bank account(s)

While the above overview does not cover all eventualities, it does contain the major areas for which money must be available at mobilization time. Certainly, the subject is important enough to warrant a more detailed examination of the various items.

Physicals are actually demanded by a number of international agencies for all consultants prior to their departure from home; medical certificates, vaccinations, and shots must accompany travel documents to many countries. Sound health care and periodic checkups of all employees and their dependents have proved to be a relatively inexpensive and worthwhile investment for any international firm.

Personnel moving abroad will have to sort out their possessions; some will be stored, others have to be packed and shipped. The services of a reputable international mover are not inexpensive. However, do-it-yourself is not good enough. In the case of taking personal automobiles along, the vehicles need to be prepared for the voyage and should be covered with full insurance.

Nearly everywhere, housing is one of the costliest overseas expenses. Throughout the developing nations and in some of the highly industrialized ones, like Sweden, apartments and houses that meet with U.S. standards of living are hard to find and extremely expensive. Landlords all over the world seem to be exceptionally smart businessmen;

rents are demanded well in advance together with sizeable deposits. It is not unusual that housing is made available only on a year-in-advance rental basis. For prolonged tours of duty, firms occasionally purchase housing for their members; normally this involves a cash transaction inasmuch as mortgages are difficult to obtain and rates of interest can be prohibitive.

American schools and other adequate educational facilities abroad frequently have no vacancies after the start of the school year. Therefore, arrangements should be made as early as possible to ensure that there will not be a last-minute difficulty with registration. Tuition fees vary in different countries. However, they are usually on the level of private schools in the United States, and in a few locations parents are required to become shareholders of school associations or to purchase school bonds. Sometimes employers take title to the shares and/or bonds. In any event, as we discuss in Chapter 5, the educational cost for a consultant's dependent is an official item of cost payable by the employer and not by the employee.

Ordering the supplies, materials, and equipment for an overseas job is a difficult task in itself, which requires considerably more effort and expenditure than setting up shop for a domestic engagement. Starting with communications, it may well be necessary to purchase telephones, telex machines, shortwave radios, and citizenband equipment. Even where these facilities can be rented, substantial deposits and installation fees can be expected. Duplicating machines, electric typewriters, calculators, and other electrical equipment operating with standard U.S. 60-cycle current should not be used where 50-cycle systems are installed. Special orders may have to be issued, requiring down payments well ahead of delivery time. Automobiles, station wagons, trucks, etc., will have to conform to the legal requirements of host governments, particularly with regard to size, weight, and accessory equipment. This may necessitate placing special factory orders for export, which are not normally handled by domestic dealers and, therefore, involve cash (and not domestic credit) transactions.

Airplane tickets for personnel and dependents; funds for per diems of employees and their families in transit, including hotel and food costs for a reasonable time prior to departure and following arrival at destination; baggage charges for personal belongings; and shipping expenses can amount to thousands of dollars.

Domestic insurance does not always cover foreign exposure. Policies will have to be amended and special risks included which need to be covered abroad. Premiums are not inexpensive.

Office space is sometimes as difficult to obtain as housing, and long-term leases with high initial deposits and prepayment of rental for a year or two may have to be anticipated.

The start-up of consulting activities in a foreign country often makes it desirable to establish local working contacts at an early date. Commercial representatives are available, for a fee, to file for and handle visa applications, import licenses, and registrations; agents may have to be retained to provide the documentation for customs clearances and to activate driving licenses, residence permits, license plates, social security registration, etc. Lawyers can be very helpful in expediting final contract and credit documents and providing legal advice in many areas, against a basic retainer plus expenses.

Finally, funds have to be on hand for import duties, tax stamps, and other local charges, which can be quite substantial. Where bonds are admitted in lieu of actual duty and tax payments, these have to be secured. We will see below that it is advisable in many cases to cover all local overseas expenses in foreign currency and, therefore, arrangements should be completed early during the mobilization stage to establish local bank accounts which require, of course, initial deposits in order to be operational.

It should be quite obvious from the above that the mobilization phase for an international engagement demands heavy capitalization. It is my recommendation that wherever possible, fully covering provisions be included in the agreements so that the front-end costs of the start-up can be billed and received without delays of any kind.

FOREIGN EXCHANGE

Overseas engagements require financial transactions in foreign currencies. Increasingly, consultants are paid for their services in local and third-country exchange. The days when billings were made out only in U.S. dollars and payments expected likewise have long gone by. Shortage of foreign exchange because of unfavorable trade balances and nonconvertibility of local moneys into international ones; special conventions between sovereign nations, among themselves and with the International Monetary Fund; loan agreements providing only offshore (foreign) cost components and not onshore (local) expenses are factors that contribute to the creation of financial conditions that impose varying degrees of limitations on the freedom of the flow of money across international boundaries. Particularly in those countries where local currency is not readily convertible into foreign exchange and where national legislation forbids the export of funds, special care must be taken to assure that fees for services rendered and reimbursement for expenses incurred can be properly received and processed.

The high demand for hard currency in some countries has created artificial markets, where one U.S. dollar, for instance, officially pegged at the exchange rate of 1 : 20, will bring sixty local units instead. While the temptation to take advantage of such a situation is great, it would be a gross disregard of the law and certainly against all professional ethics to operate in any way that does not fully conform to local law and regulations.

Since no two governments treat their respective exchange problems alike, there exist virtually dozens of different approaches, permits, prohibitions, etc., with which a foreign consultant must be familiar before he can attempt to finance a new operation. Official agencies, ministries, etc., can usually provide copies of the exact wording of legislation and in some cases general guidelines covering foreign exchange regulations. In practice I have found, however, that these are frequently difficult to interpret and hard to understand for a foreigner. My own experience therefore leads me to consult with local and resident foreign bankers in the area, most of whom are very well informed. If particularly complicated issues are at stake, then an experienced lawyer should be brought in. For general information, foreign consulates and embassies can also be quite helpful through the commercial and economic counselors.

Where a contract provides that local costs are to be paid in local currency and foreign costs in foreign exchange, an early breakdown of these should be made. The accounting system will have to be set up in such a way that these two categories can be handled entirely separately:

Local costs will generally include the following:

- Salaries and bonus for host-country and third-country staff
- Overseas post allowance
- Local vacation and sick leave pay
- Educational allowances
- Housing
- Office rentals, utilities, local transportation
- Per diems for in-country travel
- Import duties, bonds, taxes, stamp duties, etc.
- Social security and insurance premiums
- Office supplies and local purchases
- Retainers for representatives, agents, lawyers
- Bank charges
- Demobilization costs (return to home base)

Foreign costs normally consist of the following:

Salaries and bonus for expatriates
Home leave (vacation) and sick leave pay
Overhead, including applicable payroll costs
International travel and per diems
Physicals, shots, medical certificates
Passports, visas, and special permits
Storage of employees' household goods
Expert boxing and moving of personal belongings
Boxing and shipment of office supplies and equipment
Premiums for special insurance coverage
Banking charges

Except for countries with state-controlled economies, it is usually quite easy to convert hard currency like the U.S. dollar, the French franc, the British pound, German deutschmark, Japanese yen, or Mexican peso into soft currency. But it can be all but impossible to reconvert certain local moneys back into free-flowing international funds. Further, the fluctuations on the international money markets are so unpredictable and substantial at times that even a number of respected banks in several industrial countries have reported very serious losses recently. It is certainly not recommended that a consultant assume, on top of his professional responsibilities, the additional risks of foreign exchange speculations.

Therefore, ways and means have to be found to obtain foreign exchange independently of currency conversion. While there exist a great many variations and some truly complicated formulas for these transactions, which will differ, of course, from country to country and sometimes from client to client, there are a few basic approaches that can be discussed in detail:

1. The client provides the consultant with a down payment in local funds to cover onshore (local) costs during the mobilization stage.
2. The client sets up a revolving fund in local currency, which will cover all the consultant's onshore billings during the full period of his engagement.
3. The consultant borrows local exchange and repays as the client honors his billings.

The first case is relatively simple and straightforward. Mobilization costs in local currency are estimated during contract negotiations and included as "payable upon signature of contract" prior to the start-up of the works. The money is deposited in a local bank and the consultant draws against it as needed. Sometimes this kind of an advance has to be secured by a bond. Wherever this is the case, banks and insurance companies are prepared to handle such a matter. I have known individuals and firms in Latin America and the Middle East who perform this service for their associates and clients. Whatever the premium, it is usually very reasonable and can be charged against overhead and the job.

The second possibility is better for a consultant inasmuch as local moneys are being made available for the entire lifetime of an engagement and the formalities of billing, collecting, depositing, etc., can be established from the very beginning and followed through without major changes. Revolving funds are usually placed "conditionally" into a local bank account. Whenever the balance of that account reaches a prearranged low, additional moneys are deposited so that there will never exist a shortage of local operating funds. This procedure requires careful analysis in the beginning and should be monitored closely. Adjustments in the amounts of deposit may have to be agreed upon with the client, especially if there occur changes in the scope of work, delays of execution time, or overruns in cost.

The third approach is a regular banking matter which may be complicated by certain local circumstances, such as high rates of interest, demands for security, nonavailability of substantial amounts of money on relatively short notice, etc. Whenever a foreign consultant needs a local bank credit, he should be well introduced by his client and if possible by his own bank or a foreign correspondent bank. High rates of interest prevail in many developing countries; the cost of loan money must be included somewhere in the consultant's fees. Sometimes a local bank will accept a foreign exchange deposit overseas, which would guarantee the local loan but which would not be converted into local currency. At other times, arrangements can be made through international correspondents of the local bank. Branches of foreign banks established in the host country are sometimes best equipped to handle such transactions. Clients usually accept their consultants' choice as to which establishment is to handle the credit arrangements. When there is no major problem, I have often found it a good procedure to let the client propose the bank that he would prefer.

The main difficulty with foreign-local exchange separations is that it must be understood that there are limitations on convertibility and fluctuations in the value of one currency against another.

From time to time, governments of the developing countries propose to pay all their bills in local currency and to let the provider of goods and services export commodities for which foreign exchange can then be collected. These so-called triangular deals can be quite profitable for international traders who have the facilities and experience in this particular area. A few trading companies and certain industries may actually search for such opportunities; consultants in general are neither financiers nor traders and would be well advised to move very cautiously in this highly specialized area.

LETTERS OF CREDIT

Little known to the domestic service industry is the widely accepted international practice of operating with letters of credit (LCs). Since this chapter deals with financing an international undertaking, it would not be complete without some reference to LCs. However, detailed information should be secured from active international banking circles inasmuch as these credit instruments are subject to stringent conditions and must be so written that they provide the fullest possible protection to everybody concerned.

A prime condition of a letter of credit is that it be irrevocable. This means that it cannot be revoked during its lifetime. If an irrevocable letter of credit is issued in one country for payments to be effected in another, it should also be confirmed. This indicates that the issuing bank has actually transferred the funds from the point of origin to the place of payment.

An irrevocable and confirmed letter of credit has a clearly defined validity. It may be valid (in force) for three months or three years, or for whatever period the issuer validates it. The letter of credit ceases to be valid upon expiration and can only be extended by the issuing party. It can be renewed for three months or three years, but no transaction can be billed against it unless the conditions of the LC are fully met, particularly as far as timing is concerned.

Other conditions within an LC must also be complied with word by word. There should never be any doubt left as to interpretations. LC language has to be clear, and in order to collect against an LC every single condition must be met.

A simple, irrevocable, and confirmed letter of credit may state that ABC consultants, upon submittal of their approved invoices according to contract WXY and not later than Z date, shall be paid X amount of dollars. ABC consultants will have to be careful to present their billing on ABC stationery; their invoices must have all the approvals that are contained in contract WXY; the work had to be performed before Z date and the billing amount cannot exceed the contract price and the LC amount.

Letters of credit may state approximate amounts instead of specific ones. In banker's language, this means that differences of minus or plus 10 percent are acceptable. But otherwise, unless specifically stated, every condition written into the credit instrument is firm with no exceptions allowed.

The normal application of the letter-of-credit procedure is to specify payment for services performed and expenditures disbursed against presentation of invoices. That is contract language. Consultants will have to be careful that conditions written into the agreement can be incorporated into letter-of-credit opening procedure. Thought should be given to select the simplest possible approval conditions. A letter of credit, irrevocable and confirmed, is of little use if the stipulations for collection cannot be met because client approval of billings does not come forward on time. As a matter of fact, contracts should state that clients will either approve or reject billings within a determined time.

Another way to assure prompt handling of all billings and efficient handling by the banks through the letter-of-credit procedure is to agree that consultants' invoices will be paid, say, ten days after presentation of billings, unless protested by the client.

Letters of credit are comparable to insurance policies in that they must be tailored to the individual needs of each engagement. If properly set up and administered in a businesslike manner, they not only constitute safe channels of payment but also can be used as collateral for loans.

While LCs are most frequently used for international transactions, i.e., transfers of funds from one country to another, they can also be opened for payment in local currency strictly within the country of operation. Consultants in need of local operating capital will find that a letter of credit is highly regarded as security, and that, even if they are unknown to the bank, if they are backed up by an existing LC, lower interest rates are quoted than in most other circumstances for local loan applications.

CREDIT CARDS

Major credit cards are acceptable in many countries all over the world. Airplane tickets, excess baggage, and other airline charges can be covered with an international air travel card. Automobile rentals likewise may be covered with credit cards in quite a few foreign nations. Hotel accommodations, food, even supplies of one kind or another need not always be paid for in cash but can be charged. Thought must be given, of course, to the responsibility involved in the authorized use of credit cards. Should they be in the consultant's name or in the firm's name? This is a question that must be answered according to company policy and, at times, in the light of particular circumstances. It is a fact, however, that credit cards are an effective tool in the control of cash flow, and if payment is made within the grace period of billings, interest charges can be saved and the cost of money will be minimized.

It should be noted that major credit card companies generally convert charges from a foreign currency to, say, U.S. dollars not on the date that the charge is incurred but rather on the date that the charge goes into the credit card company's computer en route to billing the user. With variable currency exchange rates, the amount due from the customer in dollars, therefore, can be somewhat different, and this may cause minor accounting problems.

CASH FUNDS

As a general rule, it is wise to travel with as little cash as possible and to keep as little cash on hand as possible. Some money is always needed for travel: gratuities for porters and services, cab fares, small emergencies. Credit cards (see above) can easily absorb major short-term needs. Traveler's checks, while not inexpensive, are relatively safe and can be purchased nowadays in many different currencies. Traveler's checks, incidentally, are sometimes not convertible where credit cards are acceptable. It is well worth the consultant's attention to investigate foreign country customs and usages of these cash substitutes. Cash itself can best be obtained through local banks. International bankers will readily issue letters of introduction to identify credit-worthy customers. Travelers' letters of credit are available from financial institutions and merchant banks.

Once again it should be remembered that there are a number of countries which, for various reasons, do not permit the free flow of their currencies across international boundaries. Nations with state-controlled economies limit how much money can be taken in and out. Others demand detailed statements upon arrival and prior to departure to show what a traveler is carrying in and taking out.

Certainly, for regular business activities, cash should not be carried but should be arranged for through transfers via local facilities. Vouchers of all financial transactions, money exchanges, interest charges, declarations, etc., are important documents that should be preserved and filed.

COLLECTIONS

Since international operations are financed with working capital from income, it is necessary from the very beginning to provide promptly the facilities to collect for services rendered and expenses incurred. Agreement on billing and collection procedures is as essential as a clear understanding of other operational aspects. Provisions must be made to ensure that foreign exchange can cover offshore requirements, and local currency can pay for onshore obligations. Delays in submitting invoices can be extremely costly. Failure to receive payments on time has forced many an international consultant into a precarious position at one time or another. Foreign clients do not always realize all the implications of delays in payment; for instance, the need of a consultant to borrow local money in order to pay local salaries when local funds cannot be converted into foreign exchange. Simple penalty clauses for delayed payments often are not good enough and just as often not accepted. What is the use of a 5 percent interest charge for not paying on time, when the going local rate of interest is 18 percent and loans are not readily available? There are experienced international consultants who will not write penalty clauses providing interest for delayed payments, and would not accept these if offered by a client. Too often payments have been deferred for all sorts of unforseeable reasons, and no protective action is possible when there exist contractual provisions that overdue moneys can "eventually be paid up with interest." Of course, there are many overseas clients who are extremely sensitive about their international credit rating and will do their utmost to avoid delays and default.

While there is no 100 percent assurance that foreign collections will come through on time, it can be argued that there is no total guarantee on domestic transactions either. The real difference between the one and the other is that overseas it is much more difficult to cover temporary setbacks, and, therefore, client credit investigations prior to contract negotiations should be careful and complete.

In addition, it may be found that relatively inexpensive credit and payment insurance is available. The Overseas Private Investment Corporation (OPIC) provides policies against inconvertibility of currencies, expropriation, and the risks of war, revolution, and insurrection for certain exposures; the Foreign Credit Insurance Association (FCIA), in conjunction with the Export-Import Bank of the United States, issues insurance against commercial risks such as insolvency, substantial delayed payments of obligations, and a number of political exposures. Insurance policies protect a consultant against major losses after reasonable periods of collection efforts. Financing of international operations must still take into account the possibility of sudden but hopefully temporary collection (income) delays.

REVOLVING FUNDS

Revolving funds (RFs), similar to letters of credit, represent a bank collection facility established by the client for the consultant's convenience and use.

Letters of credit are complicated credit instruments devised to guarantee the availability of funds to cover the consultant's billings in strict compliance with the terms and conditions of his contract. Opening letters of credit usually takes considerable time, and operating letter-of-credit accounts requires careful attention to the smallest detail.

Revolving funds are established through deposits of funds into a bank account by the client to cover the consultant's anticipated periodic billings. No restrictive or complicated limitations are applied. Immediately following the drawdown of an RF's balance, the client simply replenishes the revolving fund in anticipation of the next collection by the consultant.

As no protective safeguards are built into RFs other than a client's option to stop depositing moneys, consultants are occasionally requested to provide a bond to guarantee the integrity of their RF transactions. Such bonds are easily obtained at reasonable rates and often constitute a good investment inasmuch as RF operations are extremely simple and help to reduce waiting time for the clearance of billings inherent in other types of payment procedures.

Revolving funds are mostly used for local currency transactions. As a convenience, they rate very high and should not be overlooked as a valuable credit-collection device.

WORKING WITH ASSOCIATES

Associations and joint ventures are discussed in Chapter 8 of this book. With particular reference to financing an international engagement, obligations toward partners in a foreign venture merit special attention. Joint venture agreements, subcontracts, and intercompany letters of understanding must be specific in this area, and it is recommended that internal financial agreements be closely tied to the contractual setup with the client.

The normal procedure is to work a foreign associate's cash flow into the general financing projections in direct proportion to his participation in the project. Thus, payments and collections are handled as one unit vis-à-vis the client, and the final distribution of funds becomes an internal matter for the consultants' group.

When special stipulations demand separate billings and payments for the international consultant and his local associate, the same careful consideration has to be given the partner's financial needs as the principal's. Fees and expenses have to be clearly defined, as well as collection procedures and payment schedules. It is very important that there arise no cash flow problems with or because of associations and joint ventures. Individual professionals or small firms in the emerging countries frequently are very short of capital and have limited lines of credit. This needs to be clarified at an early stage of financial planning.

Occasionally, associates are in the position of being able to render valuable assistance by providing advance host-country currency, thereby easing the foreign consultant's local exchange exposure.

Another situation that is encountered from time to time is that local partners readily finance local costs out of their own funds beyond the proportion of their participation in return for a larger share of foreign exchange income. Tax considerations, personal reasons, and the desire to be free from local restrictions may underlie such moves. There are no end of possibilities and combinations that can be considered in this connection and which may have a direct bearing on the overall financial picture. However, as in all areas of professional involvement, consultants must be careful to operate within the law of the host countries. It may be a sound practice to receive client approval of any proposed special host-country transactions, particularly if the client handles international financial institution or government agency funds for the execution of the consultant's project.

CONTROLS

Financial planning backup by effective management controls cannot be stressed enough as being of the utmost importance for satisfactory international performance and results. Because of the many variables that contribute to changes in projections and which are sometimes difficult to monitor over large distances, complicated by poor communications facilities and foreign languages, expert administrative attention should be given to all phases of financing.

Many international consultants have found it not only advisable but also indispensable to involve ranking members of their organization in a foreign engagement with particular emphasis on exercising financial control. It is not unusual today to see treasurers and controllers personally attending contract negotiations and setting up safeguards in the field.

Bank accounts should be checked and double-checked, not only at the local project office but also at regional headquarters or in the home office. Arrangements should be made for foreign bank statements to be mailed to the field and at least one other office. Since many overseas banks do not return canceled checks with their statements, separate records have to be kept for all bank drafts. When more than one currency is involved—and possibly more than just one partner in a joint venture—deposits and checks have an uncanny way of turning up in wrong accounts and need to be traced. Balances must be verified frequently.

Different banking procedures and foreign practices easily confuse the newcomer overseas; every possible effort should be made as early as feasible to obtain a full understanding and thereby full control of all financial operations. As long as it is necessary to operate accounts in the field, powers of attorney to sign checks and order transfers and drafts, etc., should be issued in accordance with the host country's laws, legalized where required, and confirmed by the bankers.

My own experience of many years indicates that no overseas venture can be expected to be successful and profitable unless very high priority is given to adequate financial administrative details and controls. This must begin as early as during the contract negotiations and continue throughout the execution of the project until final payment has been received and all outstanding liabilities, including bonds and guarantees, are liquidated.

ADMINISTERING FOREIGN ENGAGEMENTS

Since I am covering in this book consultants who work on a great variety of projects in almost any part of the world, I can only provide general guidelines which should be followed when the time approaches to administer international engagements.

From a technical point of view, domestic consulting work may be more complicated than foreign work because of sophisticated demands and cost-saving requirements. This exists despite the fact that overseas performance under multiple technical standards, more than one language, multinational rather than domestic specifications, etc., requires extra care and special attention. It is the efficiency in administration of the international consultant's organization that demands close examination, and this chapter is dedicated to techniques that have been developed and are being followed by international firms.

MANAGEMENT

A principal of a firm, a partner, or a director of a corporation should be designated as the top management representative for international work, and this individual, in turn, must have the responsibility and authority to direct the consultant's international commitments. The importance of experienced international management has been indicated in Chapter 5, "Staffing for Multinational Engagements." Regardless of positions, titles, or classifications, in order to be successful abroad, there has to be one fully responsible individual to whom matters of professional concern and administrative nature are reported. Ideally, this individual with decision-making powers is so placed in the organization of his firm that he can keep close personal control of foreign operations and thereby influence timely decisions before costly mistakes are made. It is bad enough in the domestic field when an error is committed and corrections have to be taken. Halfway around the world, poor professional judgment or a slipup in client relations not only can mean the difference between profit and loss on a particular job, but can actually damage beyond repair a firm's reputation and ability to continue to operate.

TRAVEL PREPAREDNESS

According to the size of the consultant's organization, selected members of management and personnel must be prepared to travel on short notice. Passports have to be kept current, visas applied for so as to permit hurried departures, and vaccinations kept up to date. Many experienced international consultants never travel anywhere without carrying valid passports, international health certificates, credit cards, and a reasonable supply of traveler's checks. To give one personal example, recently attending a meeting in Miami, Florida, I received a call to attend an urgent meeting in Santo Domingo. The fact that I did have my passport and vaccination certificate with me made it possible to proceed immediately, without having to return home first. Preparedness for mobility such as this pays off in client relations, and keeps costs down.

PASSPORTS AND VISAS

U.S. passports are valid for five years and are issued by the Department of State in Washington, D.C. Applications may be made to the clerk of any state or federal court. Frequent international travelers should indicate on their passport application that they intend to take many international trips, in which case, at no extra cost the passport issued to them will contain more pages than the ordinary tourist travel document. If a passport fills up with visa entry and exit stamps, additional pages can be added by American consular officials overseas or State Department passport officers in this country.

For business purposes, it is recommended that passports be applied for by individuals and not families. This will permit consultants to travel without their spouses, and children without their parents. It is easier to handle travel documents for each individual person than for family groups that may split up at one time or another for reasons which cannot be foreseen.

Tourist cards sometimes cover U.S. citizens visiting foreign lands for short periods of time; visas issued by consular officials are required by others. Work permits are a must almost anywhere when consultants' personnel have to perform professional services over a prolonged period of time inside the host country. Never travel without the proper visas and permits. Even an involuntary slipup can have serious consequences, such as loss of time, local fines, disqualification to work, etc.

When a firm has official engagements in foreign countries, governments sometimes issue courtesy or other type visas, which will permit members of the consultant's team to enter and leave the country as required. It is good policy to have these visas ready and prepared for those on the management level as well as for other employees, well ahead of the time of assignment, and even on a standby basis.

U.S. citizens should be aware of the fact that foreign visas should not exceed the validity time of the U.S. passport. If they do, difficulties arise because upon issuance of a new passport, the U.S. authorities invalidate the old one. Consequently, U.S. passports may have to be renewed at times ahead of their actual expiration time so as to obtain new valid visas for continued travel and work abroad.

OVERSEAS TRAVEL

In the execution of international engagements, consultants are required to travel frequently. For the international president, vice president of foreign operations, or head of the overseas division, whatever the title, it is recommended that trips abroad do not exceed twenty-one working days. Recent surveys conducted in several countries indicate that the traveling executive definitely loses efficiency after three weeks in the field. This applies to a somewhat lesser degree to the consultant's staff as well; but it is usually the top managers who are required to put in long hours of daytime work, in addition to necessary evening entertainment functions. A good many of my friends, when they travel from country to country, use breakfasts, luncheons, and dinners for business meetings. However, three weeks of that type of work take their toll. A quick return to the home office and some time there in familiar surroundings permits them to "recharge their batteries" before going out again.

Much has been said and written lately about the so-called time lag and the effects of international jet travel. There is no doubt that changes from one time zone to another, being exposed to a variety of climates, altitudes, etc., affect the traveler's health, general disposition, and probably more often than is recognized, ability to make sound decisions. Jet travel has varying effects on different people; some tire easily, while others claim that they rest better in flight than at home. Personally, during long journeys I like to settle down and work, especially since I find few other opportunities and places where there is less disturbance than on a plane. However, I do admit that I am as tired stepping off a plane, say, eight hours after boarding as I would be after leaving my office after putting in eight hours of work.

FIRST CLASS OR ECONOMY

Most established companies have definite policies setting forth the style in which they expect their personnel to travel and to live. Domestically, top executives are entitled to use first-class transportation with rare exceptions; a number of consultants also permit first-class privileges for long trips exceeding, say, six hours of uninterrupted flight.

International clients are generally sensitive about the high expense of first class and sometimes refuse to cover more than the cost of economy class. Consultants, therefore, should be somewhat flexible in their policies for overseas travel. Such factors as the length of trips, availability of space, ability to make reservations, and transfers from one line to another may also have to be considered. On certain Latin American routes, for instance, it is actually easier to find space in the economy section.

If there are special reasons why consultants should fly first class, the firm may have to absorb the difference in cost, which can be quite substantial. I know of cases of very tall or heavy individuals who simply do not fit into economy-class seats on most planes. Professionals with physical handicaps, also, will fare much better in more spacious seats. On the other hand, an experienced world traveler can normally adjust to the seating in the economy class.

Years ago it was prestigious to travel first class, a leftover from the days of trans-Atlantic and Pacific steamer passages. Today, one meets as many important contacts in the economy section as in first class; in fact, an increasing number of airlines use planes with only one class on international routes.

Similar thoughts and considerations ought to be given hotels abroad. Many well-known national chains have established luxurious facilities overseas aimed principally at the tourist trade. Oftentimes, these "little Americas" are out of town and require expensive taxi or rental-car transportation for the consultant to move about. Centrally located, comfortable, and clean accommodations are important. It is therefore good to find out which foreign cities offer perfectly acceptable hotels of their own, where—as a matter of fact—the foreign visitor is usually better received and attended than in the tourist-oriented international hotel, at considerable savings in rates, transportation, and time.

ALTITUDES HIGH ABOVE SEA LEVEL

High altitudes, such as in Mexico City, Bogotá, Quito, La Paz, etc., have a definite effect on travelers. Personnel should be cautioned to move slowly and to avoid excitement upon arrival. One should stay away from alcoholic beverages, heavy foods, and even smoking for the first twenty-four hours, at least.

COMMUNICATIONS

Very few businessmen need to be convinced nowadays that efficient means of communications and effective communication policies should receive top-priority attention. Within the United States, we enjoy an excellent telephone system. Despite mounting protests, the U.S. mails are still reasonably reliable compared with the postal services in other countries. Communicating internationally, however, poses problems. Telephone systems via satellites, telex, and cable connections are constantly improving, but are still far from perfect. International consultants should be alert at all times to move quickly and decisively to establish the best available systems of communications within their overseas operations.

TELEPHONES

International telephone service is quite reliable and relatively inexpensive. However, there are a number of countries where the installation of a local telephone requires long waiting periods and considerable subscriber's fees. Also, while it may be easy to telephone several thousand miles across the oceans from one country's capital to another's, it may be nearly impossible to obtain a satisfactory connection locally. Telephone facilities should be checked out overseas at an early stage of any involvement, and preparations made to avail oneself of the best possible setup. Because of occasional systems difficulties in this country and overseas, telephone listings should be available of the official office telephone numbers, as well as of the residences of principal employees, so that in case of need, communications can be maintained outside of normal business channels.

INTERNATIONAL CABLES

Cable messages, transmitted internationally via radio or trans-Atlantic cables, can be compared to domestic telegrams. As there is a charge for every word, highly specialized consultants may develop their own private cable codes whereby a combination of letters signifies whole sentences and/or indicates professional proceedings. The use of coded cables is quite customary in the foreign service among the commodity dealers and international merchants. To a lesser degree, it can be not only a cost-saving factor for a consultant but also one that ensures confidentiality of messages that could have economic and political implications. Private cable codes are forbidden only in a few countries. It is therefore a matter of judgment and an estimation of costs that will ultimately decide if an international consultant should delve into the rather extensive work of preparing codes and then training his personnel to code and decode messages.

The international communications companies accept code names in lieu of full, detailed addresses. Registration of a coded address has to be undertaken once a year in every location where the address is to be kept in force. In quite a few countries, the cable companies will also accept delivery instructions when receiving code addresses. For instance, messages received after business hours or during holidays can be directed to a private residence or for telephone transmittal, pending delivery of the printed cable when the offices open for regular business. A full understanding of international cables is quite easy; representatives of the service companies are usually available for personal explanations and printed descriptive material can be obtained.

TELEX

Telex service is one of the great innovations of our times, and I wonder sometimes how it was possible in years past to successfully work internationally without it. Whereas telephone service provides oral communications to and fro, and cable messages permit the transmittal and receipt of written communications, usually within twenty-four hours via third-party switchboards and offices, the telex enables conference setups whereby typed messages will go to and fro directly from the sender to the receiver. Telex can be used for the simple transmittal of messages or for question-and-answer sessions. As in the case of cable addresses, a consultant should register his firm and have the proper telex equipment installed in his home office. Overseas, it is not always possible to promptly obtain a telex installation, and the cost may be excessive. However, public booths are increasingly installed throughout the world from where messages can be sent and conferences can be originated. One of the earliest steps in establishing overseas communications is to fully investigate telex facilities and to set up policies and procedures that will ensure trouble-free communications to the extent that they are available.

CITIZENBAND, VHF, AND RADIO TRANSMISSIONS

Where special conditions prevent the use of traditional, public communication systems, consultants may have to devise their own. This is particularly so for local office-to-field operation communications and communications with mobile units.

The electronics industry has lately developed many two-way systems that can be employed for varying conditions and at quite reasonable cost. Special permits and operator licenses may be required, but are usually easily obtainable. Prior information on available frequencies will ensure that equipment can be properly set up.

SURFACE MAIL, AIRMAIL, AIR FREIGHT, ETC.

The mails have to be watched everywhere, including the industrialized countries. Sometimes the best-organized and most reliable mail systems simply break down because of strikers, political or labor difficulties, or natural disasters. During the earthquake in Managua a couple of years ago, dedicated Nicaraguan post office employees saved most of the mails but had considerable difficulties with the distribution. A recent protest by postal workers in Italy bogged down the mails so terribly that uncounted letters, parcels, and packages never reached their destinations. To ensure, at least, that mail is under control within the consultant's powers, international mailings should be numbered in such a way that writers and addressees are able to trace remittances. In some instances, originals should be duplicated and sent out two or more times with intervals of one or two days. It behooves a consultant to carefully investigate the various options of different services at his disposal, which also includes delivery via airlines and on some official engagements, the use of courier services and diplomatic pouches.

OVERSEAS OFFICES FACILITIES

In order to perform sound, professional work, consultants should have adequate facilities at their command to provide their services in an atmosphere conducive to creative thinking and efficient performance. I certainly do not advocate luxuriously furnished suites with all sorts of gadgets and trimmings that modern times have dreamt up, but I do believe in quiet, well-lit, properly ventilated offices where a person can enjoy spending his working hours. Enlightened management recognizes that appropriate working conditions are necessary. Contract negotiations leading to an engagement or a policy decision establishing a branch in a given area should give proper consideration to the costs involved, which may be quite considerable in certain areas overseas.

At times, consultants have little choice when a client requests that the expatriates move in with the host-country organization. A similar condition prevails when, because of local associations or joint ventures, the foreign consultant is invited to share the client's local friends' facilities. But it is different, of course, when the choice is entirely the foreign consultant's. The selection of functional offices, furnishings, and equipment should be high on the list of priorities when setting up shop overseas.

Consulting engineers are sometimes required to maintain personnel permanently on construction sites far away from civilization. Here, it pays to specify at an early date what the client or the contractor is to furnish in the line of office facilities. Self-contained, mobile-home-type trailers are becoming increasingly popular in this respect. Camp-type installations should ensure certain minimum standards, particularly offering protection against climatic conditions prevalent in the project area. Sanitary facilities must guarantee that consultants are not unduly exposed to health risks, and arrangements should be made well in advance of the start-up of work to ensure that the personal safety and security of the consultant's staff are provided for.

Consultants are frequently at liberty to propose the furnishings and equipment that they want to employ for a given assignment abroad. I recommend that before deciding to import, the local market be surveyed as to what can be obtained in the host country. Electrical characteristics should be checked. Although 110/220 volts, 60 cycles, may be standard for the United States, certainly this is not the case in a number of other industrialized nations, and even less so in the emerging world. Hence, equipment operating with electricity—starting with the expatriate's electric shaver and toothbrush to the office copying machine, the typewriter, the calculators, etc.—will have to be adaptable.

Some companies have set policies as to the makes of machines that they use. This is justified for domestic operations. Overseas, however, an experienced manager will carefully survey the local market with regard to service facilities and availability of parts. The best of the domestic makes, for which unlimited service is available at home, may last but a short time in a location where the manufacturer's service representative is not able to fully back up his firm's products.

Office security is another factor that should not be overlooked. File cabinets and safes should fully protect valuable documents. An expatriate should never forget that even a simple electronic calculator that may cost $25 at home may be the object of a break-in elsewhere.

Protection against the environment is something else that frequently escapes a newcomer in the foreign field. Heavy humidity during the rainy season can damage and destroy records in very little time; floods and inundations are commonplace in some of the world's lowlands. Civil disturbances, unexpected riots, and even open warfare have been known to interrupt international development work. How well-protected are your overseas offices against these eventualities?

VEHICLES

Consulting work requires mobility. In setting up foreign operations, it is essential to thoroughly think through and plan how to best ensure that the proper vehicles are available when needed.

The use of automobiles for everyday personal and business use is still a luxury in many countries. Economy-sized American cars are often the largest automobiles permitted in certain developing nations. Large or medium-sized vehicles would be totally impractical, if not forbidden altogether. Four-wheel drives in certain areas are a must in order to get through. To import or to buy locally is an ever-present question. Thus, the choice of a car or a fleet of vehicles requires an understanding of local conditions. Again, as in the case of equipment, it is also very important to establish if certain makes of vehicles can be serviced locally by car dealers who have trained mechanics and a supply of parts on hand.

When negotiating contracts, clients sometimes offer their prospective consultants the use of local vehicles and drivers. My personal experience dictates that this is not usually satisfactory. Too often the automobile that is needed is not available just on time, drivers have other obligations, and local maintenance and repair are not up to acceptable standards. I recommend that consultants endeavor to maintain full control over their own transportation.

TO DRIVE OR NOT TO DRIVE?

American driving licenses are usually valid and honored in foreign countries for a limited time, usually up to thirty days after arrival. Thereafter, it may be necessary to obtain local driving licenses. A number of sovereign nations also recognize the international driving license, which is issued by the American Automobile Association. However, there have been reports that these licenses are regarded as valid for tourism only, and it may be well to make quite certain that no expatriate drives without being absolutely sure that his license is valid.

Domestic U.S. insurance does not normally cover driving in foreign countries. Companies can obtain international coverage for their international staff domestically; in case of accidents and claims, however, it may be better to obtain local insurance coverage. This also makes for good local relations. Insurance company agents overseas usually belong to an influential group of businessmen who will appreciate the opportunity to write policies for foreign consultants, who are considered an excellent risk everywhere.

As everybody knows, accidents do happen, and some of these can be fatal. Under Anglo-Saxon law, everybody is innocent unless proved guilty. Roman law is directly opposite. Even in case of a simple accident, you are considered guilty unless you can prove that you are innocent. In a number of sovereign nations, fatal automobile accidents carry extremely severe punishment regardless of guilt. I can never forget the case of a most honorable Swiss citizen in a Latin American country, who was blinded at night on a narrow country road by an oncoming car and plowed into a group of men standing by the roadside, killing several of them. He was imprisoned for several months until his case came up for trial, and then condemned to support the families of the casualties for life. The unfortunate man never recovered from this tragic accident. Unable to leave the country to pursue his business activities, he finally committed suicide. A responsible consultant will have to investigate local laws and procedures regarding driving automobiles. Under certain circumstances, he will have to hire local drivers for his expatriate and third-country employees in order to escape uninsurable and, under our ways of life, unreasonable risks.

INSURANCE COVERAGE

In addition to automobile and accident insurance, local legislation and practices that develop in certain areas over the years by tradition and through experience dictate that foreigners take a good look at exposures and the insurance coverage that is available. This is not only confined to social security, accident and health, and life insurance, but also should include property and work-under-progress insurance, damage to third parties, and special conditions that may be prevalent. Kidnapping of a company employee, for instance, is something that was unthinkable up to fairly recently, but is now one of the dangers that needs consideration. Obviously, insurance against kidnapping should be taken out in a third country and with discretion and the knowledge of only the most limited number of trustworthy insiders. Otherwise a kidnapping insurance policy would, in fact, quickly become a hunting license.

BANKING ABROAD

Chapter 6 of this book, "Financing an International Operation," deals with domestic and international financing. In order to be able to set up a businesslike foreign operation properly, host-country banking connections are desirable and recommended. These should match and interphase as closely as possible with the domestic banking arrangements to which the consultant is accustomed. The opening of accounts, transfers of funds, payments of drafts, etc., have to be carefully registered and supervised. It should not be forgotten that financial controls and banking practices vary from country to country.

Large international banks have foreign branches and/or maintain relationships overseas through correspondence and representatives. Banking is a competitive business, and bankers look for customers just as consultants search for clients. Information about host-country banking facilities, therefore, is relatively easy to come by, and preliminary arrangements should be completed promptly so that basic operations may proceed when needed. Hurried last-minute arrangements can turn into costly misadventures.

Consultants may also find it beneficial to review and revise one or the other of their customary domestic procedures in order to operate more efficiently and economically in the international markets where different usages prevail.

It should be noted that corporate powers of attorney or resolutions by the partners of a firm or the board of directors of a company are required in a number of countries before bank accounts can be established and transactions started up. It may be necessary to legalize, translate, and register these documents. Local bankers or local counsel will be in the position to provide complete information concerning these details.

Banking, incidentally, is not everywhere the kind of a "service industry" to which we are accustomed in the United States. Here, deposits are the big word, and bank expenses are quite reasonable for most operations. Overseas, deposits occasionally generate a small-interest credit. On the other hand, surcharges, handling fees, stamp duties, commissions, and premiums may amount to sizable charges. A careful investigation of banking practices and procedures is very much in order before a firm commitment is made to proceed with any given entity.

LEGAL ASSISTANCE

Consultants are notorious for their occupational independence. They frequently rely too much on common sense, good judgment, past experience elsewhere—they do not readily consult with others outside their profession.

Alas, foreign business liabilities, complicated aspects of tax-related matters, labor laws, and leases—just to mention a few matters—do require expert legal advice. A local attorney should be selected at an early date and acquainted with the consultant's proposed activities in the host country. Even if immediate legal assistance is not needed, it is good to have a lawyer available on short notice. From time to time, a consultant requires a local representative to take care of corporate, financial, legal, and other related matters. Competent attorneys frequently are in the position to assume these tasks, and will do so against a retainer, or for a fee. Again, foreign practices differ substantially from those in this country, and whenever possible, all the necessary details should be investigated and arrangements concluded so that the best and most economical use from legal advice can be derived when the occasion demands it.

GENERAL OBSERVATIONS

The execution of international jobs is essentially different from domestic work in that, as is indicated above in so much detail, administrative support places heavy demands on knowledgeable, skillful management, with varying conditions from country to country.

However, attention must also be given to other important areas. Has a consultant been engaged to bring the standards of his home experience overseas? Or is he to develop something entirely new that may bring about local improvements within the environment of the host country? Reasoning and judgment are required to come forward with sound solutions to matters of ecology, demography, religious practices, and historic traditions. Frequent consultations with the clients are advisable. Where there is more than one language involved, interpretations should be examined and double-checked to make sure that there is a complete understanding of those circumstances that could appear superficial at first sight, but that might be of unexpected importance. Meetings, conferences, change orders, and any departures from agreed-upon procedures need to be recorded and confirmed in writing with notification of all concerned parties.

If the work is performed by the consultant at his home office, it may be well to invite representatives of the client to visit and discuss progress at various stages of completion: alternatively, top professionals should keep a watchful eye on developments in the field to minimize the risk of painful and costly misunderstandings.

The scope of work and the terms of reference need to be reviewed time and again. The more checkpoints built in to safeguard foreign engagements, the greater is the opportunity to complete the assignment to the satisfaction of the client. Also, closing out the books with a reasonable profit and knowing that achievement of excellence has been accomplished are the realization of all true professionals' ultimate goal.

ASSOCIATIONS, JOINT VENTURES, AND REPRESENTATION

The most advantageous and proper way to secure a contract and to render professional services abroad is a topic of never-ending discussion among international consultants. Should we associate (form a joint venture) with others, or establish a foreign partnership with host-country nationals, or appoint representatives or agents? These are some of the questions that come to mind in this connection. What are the answers?

There is general agreement that foreign consultants, mostly from the industrialized countries, are called upon to take the lead in nearly any kind of engagements in the lesser-developed nations. It follows, therefore, that project responsibility and the decisive expertise rests with the international consultant.

When consultants from one industrialized country are invited to perform their services in another developed nation, circumstances may require the foreign consultant to subordinate his activities to those of the host country. In this case, precontract discussions and final negotiations will have to determine the extent of organizational involvement that may be beneficial or required. Where the final decision belongs entirely to the consultant, which frequently happens, expediency will determine whether associations, joint ventures, or foreign partnerships should be developed.

In the developing countries, the situation is not so easy and cannot be generalized without restraints. Historically, consultants would hire whatever help they required and pay compensation in line with the then prevalent local practices and rates. Host-country participation in consulting work was minimal and mostly confined to a limited employment relationship.

Subsequent to World War II, it was found that the procedure of hiring local help directly at local rates of compensation created unhappy relationships with the foreign consultant's employees. This resulted from substantial differences in the standards of living reflected in the salaries and benefits between local employees and the overseas staff of the international consultant. Thus, in order to avoid discriminatory practices, international consultants began to engage subcontractors, preferentially host-country nationals and firms, who would enter into specific contracts with the foreign firm and then staff with their own nationals.

As development work progressed in many parts of the world during the past twenty-five years, more and more individuals in the emerging nations started to demand full participation in the direction and execution of undertakings in their respective countries. Some of these were young professionals, educated in the universities and colleges of the industrialized nations; others had accumulated considerable working experience over the years, first as employees and then as subcontractors to international consultants. As a result, new changes came about. Faced with aspirations of independence and nationalism, international consultants discovered that it was not only mandatory at times in certain countries, but outright convenient, to associate with qualified local individuals and firms.

It was also found, however, that from time to time partnerships, joint ventures, and representations were forced upon foreign firms which in the end would not be to the best interest of the host country, the client, or the consultant. Therefore, it may be well to give this subject some careful attention and consideration.

Associations, within the framework of this chapter, refer to the formation of a partnership, a company, or a corporation, and are composed of a foreign consultant and host-country individuals or firms. Associations may also include joint ventures, whereby nonresidents and locals, voluntarily or in order to comply with applicable host-country legislation, set up an entity to perform professional services. It is not intended to provide here a detailed guide to specific legal requirements or implications, for, as it happens, these will vary from country to country. However, it should be of interest to examine the available options that can contribute to satisfactory and efficient operations overseas.

ASSOCIATING FOR THE DEVELOPMENT OF NEW BUSINESS

Associations of one kind or another are sometimes formed simply for the purpose of developing new business. It is extremely difficult even for large consulting firms to fully cover the world's markets, as has been described in Chapters 1 and 2 of this book. By having a local associate monitor host-country programs, foreign consultants will be well informed of upcoming projects and therefore in the position to plan their first moves with sufficient time and at a reasonable cost.

A local partner, besides providing forthcoming project intelligence, may submit his foreign partners' registrations, where required, and prepare proposal documentation and translations, thereby saving valuable time and expenses.

When it comes to proposal presentation, negotiations, and contract work, the local associate once again plays a most important role. He knows his particular environment and customs; certainly, he can provide accommodations and transportation for his international partners; his experience will reliably indicate what elements of professional and material support are available locally for the planning and execution of the project and at what cost.

Some governments demand that foreign consultants be "represented" in-country on a permanent basis. This should not discourage anybody; to the contrary, in my experience there is no better way to cover an overseas market. Associating abroad for the development of new business, therefore, is desirable and highly recommended.

ASSOCIATING FOR THE EXECUTION OF FOREIGN ENGAGEMENTS

To enter or not to enter into a local partnership for the execution of a foreign engagement can be a complex problem. Obviously, there is no choice where host-country legislation makes it mandatory to have local participation; the consultant must incorporate host-country nationals into his team. The major task in this case is to locate competent individuals or firms who can be integrated into the undertaking with the maximum assurance of harmony and success.

When there exist no legal obligations requiring local partnerships, then the foreign consultant will have to weigh the advantages and disadvantages connected with entering into a local association. The following questions may be taken as a guide to this consideration:

Will a local partnership with host-country nationals:

- make it easier, more efficient, and more economical to execute the engagement?
- sustain the established professional standards of excellence?
- invite less or cause more local interference in the project performance?
- provide advantages for preferential selection for future projects?

The performance of professional services overseas obliges a consultant to take seriously into account host-country customs and usages. A direct link with local individuals or firms unquestionably facilitates a better understanding of the respective environment; an intelligently mounted combined operation will eliminate an otherwise frequently delaying and costly apprenticeship.

Efficiency can be stepped up through the use of a local partnership in most cases. For instance, communications, always sensitive between field offices and foreign headquarters, flow more easily with the elimination of differences in languages, measurements, standards, and timing. Even those annoying holidays that always seem to interfere with tight schedules and the visits of foreign executives suddenly cease to present problems.

Savings become possible in many areas. Time-wise, local partners are in a better position to arrange for important appointments and meetings. Logistics can be handled the "customary way"; prices will reflect local levels and not those marked up for the tourist. In areas where bargaining is a way of life, the expatriate need not fear being taken. Administrative details such as bookkeeping, accounting, billings, collections, correspondence, etc., can be entrusted to host-country nationals, enabling the expatriates to concentrate on their specialized professional tasks.

In order to uphold professional standards of excellence, the international consultant needs to assess the capabilities of his proposed local associate most carefully. On the one hand, the entire reputation of his entity is at stake; on the other, local experience and "know-how" may be of considerable benefit.

Governments of the lesser-developed world have frequently accused architects, engineers, and planners from the industrialized nations of overdesigning and underestimating projects. Will the participation of experienced locals minimize these risks? Personally, I think it becomes a matter of good management and close supervision to merge professionals from different countries into one successful team. There are many examples of excellent international partnerships where top professionals work happily side by side with their local counterparts. In these cases, the assignment of responsibilities followed a simple review of the educational background and experience of the individuals concerned.

Occasionally, consultants are requested to associate locally with individuals and firms who do not appear to be in the position to credibly execute the engagement under discussion. Nothing good comes of these "forced marriages," particularly if the foreign consultants are to be held responsible for overall performance. In such a case it is best to propose alternatives and if these are not acceptable, to decline.

Local interference in project performance at times creates difficult situations. This is the case when projects are financed by the international banks or agencies, and it occurs that national aspirations run counter to the established terms of reference and scope of work, or when governments change. There is no hard-and-fast rule to determine whether local associations invite less or cause more local interference in project performance. Each case must be looked at on its own merit. I have found, however, that a competent and truly professional local partner usually can be extremely helpful in defusing potentially explosive situations. Such a partner can also provide background information and insight leading to an understanding of events and demands which will make it easier to find a solution.

Associates with political connections are definitely not my choice. They have a tendency to attract more attention and publicity than necessary. Whenever somebody states that his connections with government, or the party in power, or a particularly outstanding politician, assure preferential consideration and treatment, I am weary. There have been too many changes of governments, resignations of leaders, and reversals of policies in my lifetime to let me place my trust in anything but the truly professional qualifications of a partner.

Consultants are generally assigned to perform specific services that will finally end at some time. As has been discussed in other chapters of this book, it is not easy to obtain work in the international marketplace. Repeated engagements from satisfied clients, hence, are most desirable. Enlightened management will give consideration to this factor as soon as plans are prepared for the execution of any foreign work. Competent and respected local partners can be extremely helpful to the international consultant as he builds a foundation for future prospects. Doors that remain closed for most outsiders will open on short notice. As foreign consultants are watched and judged through local eyes, the simple imprint of a local partner's name on studies, reports, drawings, and specifications will influence judgment. Stationery combining the name of foreign firms with local ones is living proof, particularly in the emerging nations, that the foreign consultant has cooperated closely with host-country people, and that there exist a common base, mutual trust, and confidence. This is of great importance these days in a world with expanding nationalistic trends.

A further advantage achieved by entering into associations overseas is that local partners are better able than most outsiders to obtain professional licenses, work permits, and membership in national societies. These are but three requisites to foreign undertakings that can be time consuming and costly. Local partners sometimes offer to furnish instruments and equipment, thereby saving money and eliminating the risk of breakage or loss in shipments. At other times, associates are glad to accept, in lieu of payment for services, the instruments and equipment that their foreign partner imported for the execution of the project.

Except for special circumstances, such as the injection of politics into the profession, the nonavailability of suitable local partners, the confidential nature of the project itself, or special contractual limitations, associating abroad for the execution of an international engagement may be as much recommended as the establishment of local partners for the development of new business.

DIFFERENT KINDS OF ASSOCIATIONS AND JOINT VENTURES

Foreign associations, partnerships, and joint ventures may take several forms. A number of countries have enacted special legislation limiting the options; others have chosen to provide only the barest guidelines. Legal counsel should be sought in the host country and possibly be combined with the consultant's attorney at home. Whatever the form of the association, the terms need to be clearly worked out in sufficient detail to avoid any later misinterpretations and misunderstandings. Clients may have to be consulted as to their acceptance of the proposed partnership.

Aside from the mutual obligations, compensation, sharing of profits (and losses), tax liabilities, and social obligations, such matters as disputes, arbitration, termination and assignment clauses require careful attention.

Agreements among consultants may be simple contracts covering specific engagements and limited territories, or they may be much broader, establishing exclusive rights for prolonged periods of time. For large undertakings it is not unusual to actually establish a new professional entity, with the foreign and local individuals or firms as partners, in the form of a corporation, a limited liability company, or a partnership.

Where agreements are written to provide specific services for an already existing contract, care should be taken that the clauses of the one will not conflict with the stipulations of the other.

When a foreign and a local consultant combine their efforts to obtain a project, it is not necessary, in most cases, to enter immediately into a formal contract. Instead, a simple letter of understanding or consent should specify all the general points of agreement, which can be formalized later, after the job has been received. Sometimes these letters of understanding are required by clients. Again, in this case, it is usually quite easy to work out an acceptable document by using common sense and simple language.

Associations and joint ventures are not confined to partnerships between nationals of two countries. There may be groups of four and more different firms; the *modus operandi* of overseas associations will follow no set pattern. Americans, Canadians, and West Germans may team up with Indonesian nationals for a large undertaking in Sumatra. Argentineans, Brazilians, and Italians can be found working side by side near Asunción with Paraguayan professionals. Likewise, international joint ventures are often staffed with individuals from many countries. As long as the principal objective of such mixed operations is to provide the best services for the execution of an engagement and to satisfy the client, international consultants will find many possibilities and relatively few limitations in the selection of partners, associates, etc.

WHERE TO LOOK FOR AND HOW TO FIND A LOCAL ASSOCIATE, PARTNER, OR JOINT VENTURER

The search for prospective host-country nationals as associates or partners in some parts of the world is as easy and enjoyable as it can be difficult and frustrating in others.

For the most part, consultants in all industrialized nations function similarily in offering their professional services. The internationally active ones participate in conferences and workshops abroad and are well known in consulting circles around the globe. Their professional societies maintain registrations of individuals and firms and provide information to interested parties. Trade publications carry their professional cards. Yellow pages in the telephone books list them. It is quite easy to locate international consultants in Sweden, the United Kingdom, France, Italy, Germany, and other industrialized nations.

Throughout South America and in a few Mid-East and Asian countries, competent and experienced professionals are available and can be located. However, they are not always established and organized as independent consultants. A foreign professional looking for partners may have to spot and select individuals and then help them to set up a firm or forge a team. Many Latin Americans, particularly, are superbly educated and frequently internationally experienced; their principal interest revolves around securing an opportunity to practice what they studied and to participate actively in the progress and modernization of their respective countries. One can find them at universities and colleges which serve as gathering places. Word of mouth carries fast, especially in the smaller nations, and no major effort is required to meet candidates once it becomes known that international consultants are looking for local individuals.

In most of the African nations, in some Mid-East and Asian countries, qualified professionals available to perform private enterprise services are still difficult to engage. Individuals with degrees of higher education are usually under contract to and employed by governments. Here it can be quite a problem to come upon a suitable partner. Occasionally, members of the faculty of centers of higher education can be persuaded to join in a common effort. A carefully worded advertisement in the local press may attract the attention of parents of students performing postgraduate work abroad and establish contacts. I was quite impressed at one time when an enterprising British architect systematically searched popular universities for graduating students of a particular country. He was able to employ several bright young persons immediately following graduation and then to incorporate them as junior associates in a project he was executing in the country of their origin.

Government employees in the emerging nations are generally poorly compensated and frequently anxious to become independent. It is not unusual to obtain temporary and even permanent releases from government service for host-country professionals, particularly if the consulting engagement is commissioned by the government. From time to time civil servants are able to take a prolonged leave of absence and accept an offer from a foreign consultant. Care must be taken in such cases that there develop no misunderstandings with government agencies, and that there arise no conflict-of-interest situations.

It never hurts to talk to as many people as possible when searching for host-country associates. Personally I was fortunate more than once to establish highly satisfactory relations with qualified locals upon the recommendation of the client himself, after I approached him directly for his advice. As a matter of fact, several years ago a minister of state was so pleased to recommend a personal friend of his that this procedure substantially influenced the final selection of my firm and secured the job.

Naturally, not all host-country nationals with a professional education will make good partners and associates. Some people just cannot perform well as members of a team; others are disinclined to follow directions. Screening of prospective joint venturers is even more important than interviewing employees for international engagements (see Chapter 5). Academic records must be checked as well as professional registration. Personal references should be requested and investigated. A foreign consultant must not forget that his local associate represents him and his firm. Therefore, the final selection and appointment should stand beyond any reasonable doubts.

If after exhaustive and sincere efforts no qualified host-country professionals have been found, it may become necessary to review the proposed organizational approach to a planned project. Instead of looking for professional partners, a foreign consultant may decide to confine his local association to an organization that can provide administrative and clerical support. Individuals and firms qualified to perform these service functions can be engaged nowadays just about everywhere in the world.

REPRESENTATION

Representation, as opposed to associations and joint ventures, is generally a commercial approach, whereby an international consultant appoints a local individual or company to represent himself or his firm. Frequently, as a result of local legislation demanding that consultants be fully represented locally for prolonged periods of time following professional engagements, or even preceding short lists during a selection process, representatives can be useful. While professional associations and joint ventures are always acceptable in lieu of representation, as pointed out above, qualified individuals are sometimes impossible to find in the lesser-developed countries. Thus, in order to comply with host-country requirements, consultants may be obliged to establish a local nonprofessional representative who, nevertheless, assumes certain indispensable responsibilities. Detailed written agreements should be signed, spelling out the representative's authority and responsibilities as well as his compensation.

A typical example might be a manufacturer's representative in Latin America, who, on behalf of his foreign consultant principal, submits letters expressing an interest in upcoming local projects; files documents for official registration; receives invitations to present formal proposals; and provides an authorized, dependable line of communications. Or, a trading company in a Mid-East country that can sponsor visas for foreign visitors, arrange for accommodations and transportation, and provide translation services.

Commercial representatives are much easier to find than qualified professionals. In fact, there are a great many to choose from almost everywhere. It certainly is not an unusual sight to find small offices in some foreign city, each displaying a dozen or more brass nameplates of world-renowned multinational corporations. But again, a consultant should be careful to examine the credentials of his proposed representative. He should be firmly established and well reputed. There must be no conflicts with the representation of other, competing consultants. He should be able to prove that he can, indeed, service the consultant's needs.

One more word of caution. Representatives, at times, call themselves *agents* and propose to enter into agency contracts. In quite a few countries, an agent is regarded and accountable as a fully authorized member of his principals, whereas a *representative* can act only within the parameter of his respective representation agreement. Legal advice should be sought before entering into any commitments that contain a reference to an agent or agencies. Translations from one language to another have to be particularly clear in this connection.

COMPENSATION

Associates, partners, and joint venturers everywhere around the world must be paid adequate compensation. An early agreement covering the financial details between associating consultants is important because it establishes the business side of a professional relationship.

For all successful international joint ventures, principals and partners strive to cover their costs and allow a reasonable profit. It is good policy to set up a contingency fund to provide coverage in case of unexpected reverses. Joint incentive bonuses frequently serve as an effective stimulant for excellence in performance.

Compensation may be based on actual salaries, social benefits, and overhead. There are occasions when it may be preferable to establish time rates. Expenses may or may not be treated as direct or indirect costs, according to the nature of each individual engagement. Ideally, however, all compensation clauses of an association agreement worked out among partners should be directly compatible with the conditions and terms of the governing client's contract.

Many considerations enter into final compensation packages. If a partnership is an entirely equal one, measured in terms of input of man-hours and levels of expertise, the obvious arrangement would be an even split of fees. If there are more than two associates involved, or if one party furnishes only senior staff as against numerous participants on the lower working level provided by others, then the matter of adequate compensation becomes more complex and requires careful analysis.

I have not experienced any major difficulty in reaching amicable and satisfactory agreement with professional consultants regarding payment. Occasionally there have been philosophical differences of opinion as to the value that can be attached to the professional responsibility of the lead firm, or the "real cost" of salaries including or excluding social benefits, taxes, etc. Perhaps I have been fortunate. But there has never been an occasion when a frank and thorough discussion has not produced a mutually satisfactory conclusion of formulas leading to an appropriate distribution of compensation.

Commercial representatives are accustomed to somewhat different terms of payment in return for their services. These may vary from country to country but generally consist of a monthly retainer plus reimbursement of reasonable expenses, such as postage, telex, cables, messenger costs, registration fees, stamp duties, etc. Representatives do not normally bill for their overhead, and need not be provided with incentive bonuses.

At times, international consultants are approached by individuals and firms who claim they can obtain engagements for them in return for a retainer, expenses, and a commission or finder's fee. Occasionally, these offers look convincing and are tempting. And every once in a while, such a solicitation is legitimate and can produce an engagement. However, in the vast majority of cases it will be found that a commercial representative is not in any legitimate position to develop and procure professional services contracts. Further, rare indeed is a professional consultant's compensation that can support the payment of commissions or finder's fees. Thus it can be concluded that commercial representatives employed in areas of local support are best paid with a monthly or quarterly lump sum retainer plus expenses.

ACCOUNTING AND BOOKKEEPING

Almost every sovereign country has legislation requiring income-producing enterprises to maintain books according to authorized accounting procedures. Whenever an international consultant establishes a legal entity to perform services in a host country, the minimum demands in this connection will have to be met. Clients and their financiers frequently demand the right to inspect their consultants' books. A few international development agencies stipulate that detailed records will be kept available up to five years after the completion of specific engagements. In these circumstances, there is no choice. However, if associations, joint ventures, and partnerships with host-country individuals or third-country nationals are on an informal basis, i.e., local incorporation or registration is not necessary, then internal agreement among the parties establishes the kind of accounting and bookkeeping systems that should be set up.

Wherever a foreign consultant is subject to host-country taxation, it will be in his best interest to maintain complete records and carefully file covering vouchers. When the international consultants are subject to one kind of taxation and the host-country partner to another—something that occurs quite frequently—it is obvious that special books must be kept. The same applies when billings and collections of a joint venture are consolidated vis-à-vis the client, and the partners have to arrange for their own internal distribution of funds.

Generally speaking, accounting procedures in foreign lands can be time consuming and costly. Many international consultants for this very reason prefer to forgo legal incorporation status and formalized partnership status, wherever possible, in order to escape the administrative demands of bookkeeping abroad. This does not mean that joint venturers should not keep records for the purpose of accounting and controls. However, these can be held to the bare essentials and can involve only a minimum of effort and cost.

To associate overseas or not is a matter that comes up time and again. Experienced consultants as well as newcomers to the international markets are bound to examine the advantages of joining forces with others abroad or the disadvantages of going it alone, or vice versa. It is a question that will be raised for every prospect in a new country where the consultant has not worked before, and for many repeat engagements as well. The following key "Dos and Don'ts" for successful overseas partnerships may be helpful and provide some general guidance:

Do: Carefully investigate any proposed future associates. Make sure of their standing in their community, their professional integrity, and their financial stability.

Do: Provide fast and efficient channels of communications. Designate fully qualified and capable liaison on your side and request the same from your associates.

Do: Be positive there is full understanding on policies, agreement, authority, and responsibility. Set up procedures early; do not leave important decisions for later.

Do: Strive for the highest levels of excellence in performance; demand it from your associates as you expect it from your own firm.

Do: Plan on interchange visits—just as you and your people travel to work with your associates in their country, encourage them to visit with you and your firm.

Do: Slow down to think and discuss your problems in detail. Give your associates an opportunity and time to understand and catch up.

Don't: Select anyone as an associate overseas whom you would not normally invite as a joint venturer within your own country.

Don't: Compromise on standards of performance and ethics.

Don't: Make any promises you cannot fulfill and do not demand anything from your associates that they cannot reasonably produce.

Don't: Tell your partners that you alone have all the answers. Listen carefully to their opinions. You may profit from their local experience.

Don't: Maintain two different sets of figures and books. Develop a clear and honest concept of costs, expenses, overheads, and profits, and be sure your associates understand and agree.

THE INTERNATIONAL DEVELOPMENT INSTITUTIONS AND FINANCING AGENCIES

Many of today's international consulting services are financed by the international development institutions and financing agencies. While governments of some industrialized nations have established export-import banks to stimulate the export of goods and services, assistance to the lesser-developed countries and to investors in overseas facilities is provided by a number of international organizations. The most important ones are listed with their current mailing address on pages 167–169 of this chapter.

No experienced consultant can ignore the importance of international project financing, be it conventional, institutional, or concessionary. Increasingly, investors, borrowers, and lenders extend their influence into the decision-making process covering large multinational undertakings.

Who is it that engages a professional consultant performing professional services in the international market when the project is internationally financed: the client, the borrower (who may be the client's government), the lender (an international development institution, perhaps)? What is the exact role of the various institutions and agencies, and how do they function? Are there any provisions (and is there protection) for the independent consultant in private practice who is faced with responsibility only to his client, but charged to follow practices and procedures that are neither his own nor necessarily those of the client? What of the relationships: consultant to client, consultant to financier, financier to client vis-à-vis the consultant?

This chapter deals in considerable detail with the international development institutions and financing agencies as they affect the overseas consulting community. Much of the information given below has been furnished by these various organizations, for they are as anxious as the consultants to develop understanding and establish goodwill to serve the best interest of all those involved in international cooperation.

Most international agencies commissioning and requiring consulting services are related in some manner to the United Nations. Let us look at a number of these as they function in combination with the United Nations Development Programme.

UNITED NATIONS (UN)—NEW YORK, NEW YORK, U.S.A.

The UN contracting activities include surveys and feasibility studies for the utilization of mineral, geothermal, surface, and ground water resources; transport; hydrographic studies, water management, and flood control; power development, geophysical surveys, mapping, and training; research and training for urban and regional planning and housing construction; national and regional economic and social development planning and implementation; public administration and strengthening of government services; tourism studies; oceanographic studies; computerization; and harbor and port studies.

Parties interested in UN projects must complete and file a technical-data questionnaire and punch card with the Purchase and Transportation Service of the UN. The information is then registered in New York and long lists are compiled from this roster. Short lists are developed for a particular project by a special task force. An advisory panel composed of representatives of the Technical Operation, Purchase and Transportation Service, and the Substantive Office reviews each short list prior to the release of a call for proposals. Short lists are normally composed of five or six firms.

INTERNATIONAL LABOUR ORGANISATION (ILO)—GENEVA, SWITZERLAND

The ILO sets up vocational training schemes; trains vocational instructors, supervisors, and specialized personnel; is interested in management development and strengthening of productivity and other means for raising output; improvement of the occupational environment; advisory services for crafts and small-scale industries; assistance in personnel planning and employment promotion.

To be placed on the ILO roster, interested parties must submit detailed reports on their fields of activity and previous experience in training programs conducted in developing countries. Long lists are derived from the roster. Those longlisted are sent a model contract with project details and specifications and are invited to tender their interest. A short list is drawn from these tenders. Those on the short list are then invited to negotiate an agreement at the ILO head office.

FOOD AND AGRICULTURE ORGANIZATION (FAO)—ROME, ITALY

The FAO is concerned with studies for the development of the basic soil and water resources for agricultural development; promotion of the global exchange of new and improved plant species and their introduction; the spreading of advanced agricultural techniques; the expansion and improvement of animal husbandry and the combating of animal diseases; the development and utilization of the resources of the sea; applied research in nutrition and food science; soil erosion control; the expansion of training and extension services; processing, storage, and marketing of agricultural, forestry, and fishing products; the improvement of hides, skins, and leather production; land reclamation and resettlement; pilot schemes and demonstration projects in the field of rural development; development of forest industries; irrigation engineering; control of agricultural pests and diseases and use of fertilizer; and socioeconomic studies related to rural development.

Interested parties should register with the Chief of the Contracts Branch of the Administrative Services Division in order to be included in the FAO's register of consultant firms, institutes, and/or organizations. Unless exceptional circumstances exist, contracts are awarded on the basis of international competition. Where the contract is for such matters as charter of aircraft, aerial photography, topography, drilling, or the procurement of specially constructed equipment, such as vessels or pilot plant installations, sealed bids are requested. The list of consultants to be invited is determined in discussions with the Technical Office requesting the services and the recipient government.

Where the contract services required concern professional consulting services for economic and feasibility studies where precise specifications cannot be established, uncosted technical proposals are solicited. Invitees for proposals are restricted to a short list of three, which is approved by an interdepartmental committee of the organization and the recipient government. In determining the list of firms to be invited, primary consideration is given to those firms, institutes, and organizations that are registered with the FAO and have submitted expressions of interest in carrying out the proposed contract.

UNITED NATIONS EDUCATIONAL, SCIENTIFIC AND CULTURAL ORGANIZATION (UNESCO)—PARIS, FRANCE

UNESCO is dedicated to the improvement of education, school development, and teacher training; science teaching; youth activities and adult education; educational mass media; work-oriented adult literacy pilot projects; scientific and engineering education and technical teacher training at the university level; support of polytechnic schools; applied research centers; hydrological studies and power engineering research; oceanography; life sciences; planning of science policy; creating infrastructures and training of mass media; assistance in establishing communication policies; peace and human rights; social sciences; and preservation of monuments and international standards.

On receipt of a letter expressing interest, the Bureau of Relations with Member States and International Organizations and Programmes acknowledges its receipt and routes it to one of UNESCO's four program sectors: education, science, communication, and culture (the principal interests being education and science). The firm is then added to rosters kept by sectors which are charged to have a basic knowledge of major organizations and firms with prerequisite capability, and these are contacted for competitive proposals when terms of reference have been developed. A project description is then drawn up that details the respective roles of UNESCO and of the consultant. Files of potential consultants are reviewed, and a short list of qualified organizations is prepared. In establishing it, the demonstrated competence of a firm is most important.

WORLD HEALTH ORGANIZATION (WHO)—GENEVA, SWITZERLAND

The WHO is established to strengthen health services; to develop health manpower; to control communicable diseases; and to sponsor environmental health and research in health. Principal fields for contracting consultant services are preinvestment studies for water supply and waste disposal and drainage; air, water, and soil pollution;

public health engineering research; and occupational health. Other areas covered from time to time: surveys for communicable disease control; undergraduate and postgraduate training for the medical and other allied professions, including sanitary engineers, nurses, medical assistants, and technicians.

In the engineering and managerial field, WHO keeps a general roster of consulting firms. Interested parties are required to fill out a WHO questionnaire in order to be listed. For individual projects, long lists are drawn from the roster. A WHO committee then selects a short list of potential consultants and, following clearance by the recipient government, requests them to submit technical proposals. These proposals are then studied and the best submission is selected on the advice of a Secretarial Selection Committee. Terms of the contract are refined in later negotiations.

INTERNATIONAL BANK FOR RECONSTRUCTION AND DEVELOPMENT (IBRD)—WASHINGTON, D.C., U.S.A.

IBRD, commonly referred to as the World Bank, and its affiliate, the International Development Association (IDA), do not limit their role to granting loans. They also provide a wide range of technical assistance services to the developing countries in such fields as economic planning, public utilities (electric power, telecommunications, water supply, and sewerage), transportation (roads, railways, harbors, airports), agriculture, industry, mining, tourism, urban planning, population, nutrition, and development banking.

For projects financed by the United Nations Development Programme (UNDP), the bank group usually utilizes the services of consulting firms and organizations in connection with technical assistance and preinvestment studies. Long lists are drawn from consultations with the government agencies involved, a review of data from the Bank's general roster of consultants, and expressions of interest. Three to five names are shortlisted, with qualifications, experience, and national origin (to achieve geographic distribution) among the selection criteria. Selection is made solely on the Bank's evaluation of the proposals, with emphasis on the potential subcontractor's experience in the field of study, the adequacy of the proposed work plan and approach, and the qualifications of the personnel assigned to the study.

Because the World Bank is by far the most important of the international financial agencies, it may be well to describe IBRD activities, procedures, and general policies in detail following the rundown of the UNDP agencies.

INTERNATIONAL TELECOMMUNICATION UNION (ITU)—GENEVA, SWITZERLAND

The ITU's field of activity is planning, regulating, and coordinating telecommunications of all types and setting up worldwide recognized technical standards; national, regional, and world telecommunications network planning and surveys; training, research, and test centers for telephone, telegraph, radio, sound, and TV broadcasting, electronics and data transmission, and technical advice and expertise to member countries.

In years past, ITU has engaged relatively few outside consultants. More recently, however, as a result of expanded activities, the utilization of consultants has taken on a more important role. To ensure a wide geographical representation of firms and professional bodies to be considered for contractual work, the ITU has established and maintained an up-to-date register of consultants and firms grouped according to their specialized fields of competence. To assess their qualifications, these firms and consultants are asked to send ITU an indication of the scale of the operations, recent and major projects successfully completed, and details of the specialized aptitudes of their professional staff. Because of the variety of telecommunication fields, consulting firms must have experience in the kind of work required for a particular project in order to be considered. Although having no commercial connection with manufacturing firms is one of the criteria generally imposed when selecting consultants, certain special exceptions have been made and will continue to be made when it is imperative that a consulting firm have production capabilities or connections with a manufacturing firm.

INTERNATIONAL ATOMIC ENERGY AGENCY (IAEA)—VIENNA, AUSTRIA

The IAEA seeks to accelerate and enlarge the contribution of atomic energy to peace, prosperity, and health throughout the world. It is concerned with studies and training programs involving nuclear power and reactors; nuclear engineering and technology; prospecting, mining, and processing of nuclear raw materials; use of radiation sources and radioisotopes in agriculture, industry, hydrology, and medicine; and safety in nuclear energy and environmental protection, as well as the international nuclear information system.

IAEA contracts to consultants have been minimal in the past but are becoming more important as a result of expanded activities. Invitations to tender are sent out to those firms known to the agency as having technical competence in the field concerned. Consultants who wish to be included in the IAEA roster should write to Vienna with informative letters and explanatory literature describing their activities and competence.

UNITED NATIONS INDUSTRIAL DEVELOPMENT ORGANIZATION (UNIDO)—VIENNA, AUSTRIA

UNIDO is involved in general surveys and studies; project identification, preparation, evaluation, design, and implementation; manufacturing technology; product handling; management services; establishment of pilot plants and industrial estates; maintenance and repair; manufacturing industries in food processing, beverage, textile and garment, leather, wood processing, pulp and paper, petrochemical and plastics, industrial chemicals and fertilizer industries, pharmaceuticals industry and other chemical products, rubber, nonmetallic mineral products and building materials, iron and steel, nonferrous metal; metal products and machinery; transport equipment, precision instruments; mining; utilities; communications; and other public services.

UNIDO maintains a roster of consulting organizations wishing to participate in its activities. Registration is based on a completed questionnaire kept in a special project file. The registration of consulting organizations and expressions of interest are prime elements in the selection of firms for the eventual invitation of contractual proposals. Requests for registration and expressions of interest relating to contracts for UNIDO projects should be sent directly by interested consultants to Vienna. A preliminary list or long list of invitees is established on the basis of (1) the consulting organization being registered with UNIDO and providing the type of service and kind of activity required and (2) firms that have written to UNIDO expressing interest in the particular project.

The short list of invitees is composed of five to ten organizations considered best qualified for the execution of a project, with due consideration to geographical balance and utilization of UNIDO's financial resources. UNIDO's practice is to invite costed proposals, based on a standard form on which the invitee indicates man-month costs in the project area and home office and expenses for subsistence, travel, and reports. Proposals are analyzed technically and contracts are awarded on the basis of the lowest acceptable proposal, the primary factor being the technical acceptability of the recommended proposal.

UNITED NATIONS DEVELOPMENT PROGRAMME (UNDP)—NEW YORK, NEW YORK, U.S.A.

The UNDP fields of activity cover projects that do not fall directly within the field of competence of any particular agency; multidisciplinary projects; new technology; regional or physical planning; and projects that governments might wish UNDP to implement directly.

Most of UNDP's projects are given out by contract to professional firms or service organizations. UNDP does not maintain a roster, but relies on data banks of other agencies, particularly the United Nations and the World Bank. The short list is normally limited to three to five firms, subject to government clearance. The firms are chosen on the basis of highest technical competence of those having expressed an interest. In cases where time is deemed too short for the information to be disseminated, UNDP will solicit informal expressions of interest before drawing up the list. Evaluation of proposals is made on the basis of specific competence, the two main factors being the quality of the staff proposed and the plan of work envisioned by the firm. UNDP uses the two-envelope system when requesting consulting proposals.

THE INTERNATIONAL BANK FOR RECONSTRUCTION AND DEVELOPMENT (IBRD) AND THE INTERNATIONAL DEVELOPMENT ASSOCIATION (IDA)

As mentioned above, the IBRD with its affiliate, the IDA, is currently the largest organization of its kind in the world. Respectfully referred to as the World Bank, or simply the Bank, the group's lending and investment commitments totaled US$6,108,000,000 in 1975. It is because of the IBRD's unique leadership position in the international financing area that it is particularly interesting to examine closely its general policies and procedures as related to consulting services, with particular emphasis on economics, architecture, and engineering. While the World Bank periodically reviews and updates its official guidelines for borrowers and consultants, they can be broadly grouped into the following three categories: (1) preinvestment studies, (2) detailed engineering and design, and (3) supervision.

Categories of World Bank Consulting Services

1. *Preinvestment studies*—the investigations that normally precede a final decision to go forward with a project. These studies may have as their objectives: (a) to establish investment priorities, (b) to determine the basic features and the feasibility of international projects, or (c) to define changes in governmental policies, operations, and institutions necessary for the successful implementation or functioning of investment projects. Studies for objective (a) include basic resource inventories, river basin surveys, and studies of alternative development patterns and of factors on a regional or countrywide scale. Studies for objective (b) include the functional design, site selection, and physical layout of specific projects, preliminary engineering and cost estimates, and the financial and economic analysis required for project evaluation. Studies for objective (c) include analysis of project-related organizations, administrative problems, planning machinery, regulatory and marketing policies, manpower resources, and training requirements.
2. *Detailed Engineering and Design*—the technical, economic, or architectural work required to fully define a project. This normally includes the preparation of specifications, contract documents, and detailed cost estimates, and often includes services in connection with the analysis of bids and recommendations thereon.
3. *Supervision*—normally comprises the field inspection of construction and/or the factory inspection of manufacturing processes during the execution of projects, the certification of invoices submitted by contractors and suppliers, and technical services connected with the interpretation of contract documents and with changes in the project that may be found necessary in the course of the work. Where appropriate, supervision also includes the coordination of work by various contractors engaged in different parts of a project and training activities for institutional development. In some instances, it may extend to services related to the start-up of facilities and their operation for an initial period.

Categories of Consulting Firms

Of the various kinds of consulting firms the bank groups' borrowers may use in connection with the services outlined above, engineering firms are most frequently required. These firms fall generally into the following categories:

1. Firms of independent consulting engineers
2. Firms that combine the function of consulting engineer with those of contractors, or that are associated with, or affiliates of, or owned by contractors
3. Consulting engineering affiliates of manufacturers or manufacturers with departments of design offices, offering services as consulting engineers

Firms in category (1) are acceptable providing their qualifications are suitable for the work in question. Firms in categories (2) and (3), even though qualified, are acceptable only if they agree to limit their role to that of consulting engineer and will disqualify themselves and their associates for work in any other capacity on the same project. In the case of category (3) firms, it is doubly important to maintain safeguards, to ensure not only that affiliates will be disqualified from future bidding on any part of the project, but also that specifications will be impartial and suitable for competitive bidding on an international basis.

The Consultant's Clients

World Bank group borrowers are required to employ consulting firms whenever their own professional resources are judged to be inadequate for the task at hand. Contracts of consulting firms so employed are normally with the borrower or with an agency designated by the borrower. These cases constitute by far the largest proportion of consulting services in which the bank group has an interest. The World Bank group also requires the services of consulting firms in connection with technical assistance financed by bank grants and preinvestment studies financed by the United Nations Development Programme, whenever the Bank is the executing agency of UNDP. In these cases, firms contract directly with the Bank, which in turn has separate agreements with recipient governments covering their counterpart contributions and other obligations. Such contracts constitute a very small proportion of the consulting services in which the World Bank group has an interest.

Defining the Consultant's Tasks

For consulting services relating to preinvestment studies in which the bank group is involved, the scope of consultant work is usually defined in considerable detail. The Bank group and its borrowers collaborate in the preparation of the budget and the terms of reference prior to the invitation of consultants. In formulating the terms of reference, agreement is reached on (1) a precise statement of the study's objective, (2) an outline of the scope of work, defining each major task to be performed, and (3) data, facilities, and services that the borrower will provide to the consultant. Terms of reference and the budget are normally based on considerable research, including review of all previous studies in the area, discussions with responsible government agencies on alternative study approaches, and assessments of data availability. Terms of reference for preinvestment studies are used by the Bank group and its borrowers for three purposes:

(1) To reach agreement among all parties concerned on the objectives and scope of a proposed study

(2) To inform consultants of the intended scope of work when they are invited to submit proposals

(3) To serve as definition of consultant services in the contract to be negotiated after final selection of a firm

In the phases following preinvestment studies, it is usually a simpler matter to define the consultant tasks since the basic characteristics of the project and related problem areas are then known. A consulting firm appointed to prepare final design and contract documents is responsible for the accuracy and suitability of its work and no modification should be made in the contract document it has produced without the firm's consent. In most cases, such firms will act as advisers to borrowers on all technical problems, with authority to make final decisions within such limits as may be prescribed by the borrower. However, consulting firms are given an opportunity to raise matters of professional judgment with the bank.

Continuity of Consulting Services

The duties of consulting firms in connection with a project financed by the World Bank group depend on the circumstances in each case.

They often include all three of the categories that were mentioned above: (1) preinvestment studies, (2) detailed engineering and design, and (3) supervision. But in some cases, preliminary work may have been satisfactorily prepared by the borrower before the project is submitted to the Bank group for consideration, and the consultant firm will then be limited to categories (2) and (3).

If a firm has carried out preinvestment studies for a project and is technically qualified to undertake the detailed engineering design and supervision, there are usually many advantages in appointing the same firm to carry through the functions (1), (2), and (3). The most important of these will be a consistency in basic technical approach and a commitment to the project cost estimate on which the investment decision was based. A new firm, upon being retained for detailed engineering only, might wish to make an elaborate review or even to repeat the preliminary design work and cost estimates done by another firm.

There have been cases, however, in which preliminary design and engineering were found to be unsatisfactory; in others, a second firm, after being retained, made major improvements on a project design. To allow for this eventuality, the option to change firms between the preinvestment study and the next stage is always left open to the borrower.

It is normally essential that functions (2) and (3) be carried out by the same firm to ensure that contract documents are interpreted properly during the project implementation stage and that modifications in design, if found necessary in the course of construction, be technically sound and in accordance with original concepts.

The Role of Government Agencies

Whenever the World Bank group is involved at the preinvestment study stage, one of its primary concerns is the involvement of the borrower and/or responsible government agencies in the study process. To the extent possible, borrowers and government agencies are asked to assign counterpart staff to work with the consultants on a full-time basis, the functions of such being:

(1) To provide liaison between the consultant and government agencies and to direct the consultants to all available sources of data

(2) To receive training in the field of the study, through day-to-day exposure to the work of specialists

(3) To discuss and review with the consultants all findings and recommendations before they are presented to the government in the form of a report

The functions of the counterpart staff are to be considered as separate from the other services the government need supply in support of the consultants.

For services in the detailed design and supervision stages, the World Bank group's primary interest is to ensure that the responsibilities of the consultants are clearly understood by the borrower and all other interested parties. Discussions are normally held to make sure not only that the consultants are aware of the terms and conditions of their engagement, but also that the borrower is aware of the responsibilities and authority that the consultants are to have on his behalf. During these discussions, the Bank normally makes clear any requirements it may have in regard to the work and satisfies itself that the borrower will give the consultants official power and discretionary rights to exercise these responsibilities and carry out the terms of the contract.

Policies and Procedures in Normal Cases Where Consultants are Retained by Borrowers

When borrowers are to employ consultants, the Bank's general rule is to leave to the borrower the responsibility for selection, administration, and supervision of the consultant. Borrowers are clearly informed that the choice is theirs and that the Bank's responsibility is only to determine whether the proposed consultants are qualified for the job and whether their conditions of engagement are satisfactory.

Borrowers accustomed to using consultants will ordinarily have no difficulty in choosing a particular firm or in preparing a list of firms. Borrowers without much experience in such matters may prepare a list from recommendations by qualified sources such as other employers or national associations of consulting firms. When borrowers have prepared lists, they are submitted to the Bank to ensure that the proposed work is within the capability of the firms listed. The employment of domestic firms is encouraged where such firms are found to be qualified, either alone or in combination with foreign firms. However, compulsory joint ventures or associations between foreign and domestic firms are not favored by the Bank.

Borrowers are encouraged to follow the Bank's published procedures for selection of their consultants. While it is considered desirable that borrowers follow these procedures, the Bank has no binding requirement to this effect. In particular, if the borrower prefers a specific firm, and the firm is well qualified, it will not be forced to consider others. In cases where borrowers prepare lists of possible consulting firms, the Bank encourages them to make the list internationally representative with, say, not more than two firms from one country, thus giving borrowers the benefit of diversity of background and national origin.

In some countries, borrowers are required either by law or by general administrative regulation to invite price proposals for consulting services. In these cases, the borrower is requested to instruct the consultants to enclose the price information in a separate sealed envelope to be opened only after the qualitative evaluation of the proposals has been completed. The Bank's acceptance of the consulting firm to be employed by the borrower and of the terms and conditions of employment rests essentially on a judgment of the following:

(1) The firm's experience, background, and general organization for the work to be performed; the adequacy of its work plan for the project; and the qualifications of the personnel available

(2) The definition of the consultant's scope of work and the allocation of responsibility and authority between the borrower and the consultant

(3) Other terms and provisions of the contract, which must be reasonable and appropriate for the type of work to be performed

Policies and Procedures in Exceptional Cases

Bank participation in the selection of consultants by borrowers beyond that outlined above is considered exceptional and is undertaken only after suitable discussion and clearance within the Bank. The mere desire on the part of the borrower to be assisted by the Bank is not a sufficient reason for the Bank to play a role in the selection. World Bank staff are instructed to avoid situations in which the Bank is used by borrowers as a protective shield.

Consultants Retained by the World Bank

As mentioned before, the Bank contracts directly with consulting firms for studies financed by Bank grants and studies for which the

Bank is the executive agency for the United Nations Development Programme. The procedures for these cases are designed to ensure that the Bank's selection of consultants is based on sound judgment and to record the decisions made. A summary outline of these procedures is given below and provides an interesting insight in the care that the World Bank group is taking in this connection.

Summary Outline of Bank Procedures

For the purpose of consultant and for related functions, the Bank sets up a selection committee consisting of the director and other staff of the project department concerned and the deputy director or associate director of projects, who acts as chairman. The procedure is then as follows:

(1) The projects department responsible for the study prepares a draft and terms of reference and, after consultation with the consultant services officer, proposes a list of capable firms, based on (a) discussions with the government agencies involved, (b) a review of available data, and (c) inspection of the project area.

(2) The committee considers, modifies if necessary, and eventually approves the terms of reference and shortlists three to five firms.

(3) The committee's recommendation is sent to the government for comment and approval.

(4) Government suggestions of improvement to the terms of reference and/or the justified objections to the list of firms are considered, but the committee generally resists unreasonable increases in the number of firms, which could reduce the likelihood that serious proposals will be submitted.

(5) After the government agreement has been received, invitations for proposals (without financial terms) are prepared and sent by the project department to the consultants on the agreed short list.

(6) Proposals are evaluated by the projects department on the basis of the firm's experience in similar projects and environment, the proposed program of work, and the qualification of staff to be assigned. The project department ranks the proposals in order of merit.

(7) The committee meets to review the recommendation and reach a decision on the final ranking of the firms.

(8) The project department then requests a financial proposal from the firm selected as Number 1 and invites representatives for contract negotiations in the Bank's Washington office.

(9) If the negotiation with the first selected firm is unsuccessful, the firm next in ranking is asked to come in for negotiations and submit a financial proposal.

Preparing the Short List of Consultants

The Bank normally invites three to five firms to submit proposals for one study assignment. Several sources are used in compiling the short list. One is a review of the firms that have expressed an interest in providing the services. Another is the Bank's own file of international firms with capabilities in various fields. Special consideration is given to firms that are known to the Bank to have satisfactorily performed similar services in the same country or region and to firms that submitted good proposals in response to previous invitations but were not successful in being selected. Another source may be the recipient government or agency, which is requested to comment on the Bank's proposed short list and may suggest deletions or additions based on its own experience with consultants that have done work in the country. As an international organization, the Bank normally invites groups of professionals of different national backgrounds. Among the firms invited for any one assignment, no more than two are usually of the same nationality.

Invitations to Submit Proposals

When agreement has been reached between the recipient government and the Bank on the terms of reference and the short list of consultants, the Bank proceeds with the invitation to consulting firms. A typical letter of invitation is usually accompanied by two separate documents, one being the terms of reference and the other consisting of supplementary information to consultants.

In the supplementary information to consultants, the Bank provides the general requirements for submitting proposals and indicates the items on which primary emphasis will be placed in the evaluation of proposals. This information includes the total number of man-months of expert time estimated by the Bank for budget purposes. While individual firms are free to increase or decrease the man-months for a given assignment, it is considered important to inform all invited consultants of the total amount of effort contemplated for the study. The Bank does not request financial information in its invitation to submit proposals. The selection of firms is based solely on the Bank's evaluation of the firm's capabilities and the qualification of their staff. Financial matters are not discussed with the consultants until one firm has been selected for negotiation of a contract.

Since it is desirable in most cases that the invited consultants have first-hand knowledge of the country of the study prior to submittal of their proposal, time must be allowed for a field visit of reasonable duration. In the Bank's practice, it has been found that forty-five days is an adequate time interval between the mailing of invitations and the due date of proposals. Under special circumstances, extensions of time are granted to all invited firms.

Proposal Evaluation

Proposals received by the Bank in response to invitations are evaluated in three categories:

(1) The firm's general experience in the field of study

(2) The adequacy of the proposed work plan and approach

(3) The personnel proposed to be assigned to the study

The relative importance of these three categories will vary with the type of study and the type of firms invited to submit proposals. Normally, the quality of available personnel is given a weight of more than 50 percent in the total rating. As a guide in evaluating proposals, numerical readings are used, which are then tabulated on a summary evaluation sheet.

To assess the qualification of personnel, the curricula vitae of key staff members proposed to work on the study are analyzed, and individuals are evaluated in the following three categories:

(1) General qualifications: education, length of experience, type of positions held, etc.

(2) Adequacy for the project: the person's suitability to perform the duties to which he or she is to be assigned for the particular study

(3) Language and experience in the region: the person's background in developing countries similar to the country in which the study is to be conducted, and linguistic ability.

The evaluation of personnel is made by members of the Bank staff in the projects department responsible, who have worked in the country in which the study is to be undertaken.

Form of Contract

After the evaluation of proposals has been completed, the Bank invites the selected firm to Washington for negotiations. In this invitation, the consultants are advised of any special problems found in the proposal review that should be discussed during negotiations; also, the firm is informed of the financial data to be submitted during the negotiation and of the general form of contract the Bank intends to use for the services.

For consulting services in preinvestment studies, the Bank normally uses a form of contract which stipulates "agreed fixed rates" for each man-month of expert time and a ceiling amount within which the study must be completed. Separate rates are determined for all experts employed in the services and for work in the field and in the home office. In addition to the "agreed fixed rates," the contract provides for reimbursement at cost for travel, equipment acquisition, and other items required for the services.

This form of contract is particularly well suited to the manner in which the Bank selects consultants since it obligates them to provide the expertise that served as the basis of their selection.

Contracts include a bar chart indicating the periods of time in which each member of the consultant team will work on the study in the field and in the home office. Under the terms of such contracts, consultants are permitted only minor adjustments in the time allocation for each expert, unless the prior approval of the Bank has been obtained. Bank contracts with consultants normally provide for payment in accordance with a schedule, following each month of the estimated duration of the study. This reduces financing costs to the consultants and should result in lower man-month rates than those that would apply under most other payment procedures.

Contract Negotiations

Negotiations, typically, start with a discussion of (1) terms of reference, (2) the comments made by the consultants on the scope of services, and (3) the consultant's proposed work program. Thereafter staffing is discussed and preliminary agreement is reached on the staff bar chart. Occasionally, to improve the quality of the team, the Bank suggests that substitutions be made for some of the proposed staff members.

This is followed by discussion of the foreign currency budget. The consultants are requested to submit a breakdown of the proposed agreed fixed rate for each person on the team. The elements of these rates include the basic salary of the staff, the social benefits payable by the firm, the firm's overhead, and the firm's fee. For extended periods of time in the country of the study, a component for overseas allowances may also be included. In addition, agreement is reached on local currency expenditures, which include a subsistence allowance and reimbursement for other incidental expenditures to be made by the consultant in the country of the study.

The Bank considers it highly desirable that an authorized representative of the recipient government participate in negotiations, since it may otherwise be difficult to reach agreement of the "in kind" services and facilities that the government will provide. It is important that all concerned have a clear understanding of the government's supporting activities (such as types and numbers of staff, offices, and local transportation) and of the counterpart the government will assign to the study.

Contracts between the Bank and the consultants are normally signed shortly after the conclusion of negotiations. The contract may be effective on signatures, at some other agreed date, or upon effectiveness of an agreement between the Bank and the government concerned. Consultants are usually allowed about thirty days after the effective date of the contract to mobilize their team in the field.

Supervision of Consulting Services

When the contract is between a borrower and a consulting firm, the borrower assumes full responsibility for supervising the consultants. In the course of preinvestment studies and detailed engineering for projects that may ultimately be financed by the Bank, Bank staff may visit the project area as part of their normal project preparation activities. However, such visits would be solely for the purpose of exchanging views on progress of the work, reviewing the consultant's interim findings, and, if necessary, assisting borrowers in resolving problems which may have occurred in the course of the work. These visits do not in any way relieve borrowers of their preliminary responsibility for the supervision of the consultant. In the course of construction work on Bank group-financed projects, the same would apply except that Bank staff will normally visit the area in which the consultants work at regular intervals in the course of the staff's scheduled project supervision activities.

Throughout the project cycle, Bank staff concerned with the appraisal and supervision of Bank-financed projects will review and judge the adequacy of the work of the consultants retained by the borrower. Their comments and evaluations are normally incorporated in regular project supervision reports, which are retained for future reference in the office of the consultant services officer.

When the Bank acts as the executing agency for the UNDP or administers Bank grant-financed preinvestment studies, the Bank contracts with the consultants and carries all responsibilities associated therewith. However, the Bank is not in a position to provide continued supervision of consultants except in locations where it has resident missions. Therefore, continued supervision of the consultant field work is normally exercised by the government's counterpart staff, who are assigned on a full-time basis whenever possible. Invoices for the services performed by the consultants are approved by the government before being presented to the Bank.

In addition, the Bank's Projects Department staff is kept informed by periodic progress reports prepared by the consultants and submitted simultaneously to the government and the Bank, and by supervision missions. As in the case of borrower-financed studies, such missions are scheduled at intervals, depending on the complexity and duration of the study. Short studies of simple subjects may require only one supervision mission while field work is in progress, while longer, more complex studies may receive three or four supervision missions.

The UNDP resident representative in the country of the study has residual responsibility to monitor, on behalf of the UNDP, the work on studies financed by that agency. To facilitate this, consultants are expected to maintain contact with the resident representative and provide him with a copy of each report prepared. However, the resident representative has no authority to act on behalf of the Bank or to instruct consultants on matters relating to their contract with the Bank.

In recent years, UNDP-financed studies have been subject to midterm reviews conducted jointly by representatives of the government, UNDP, and the Bank. On this occasion, the scope of the work as outlined initially in the study budget provided by the UNDP and the government is reviewed in the light of the consultant's findings after completion of approximately half the work program. Adjustments in study scope, schedule of operations, and budget can be made on this occasion if found necessary by the government, UNDP, and the Bank.

Final reports of consulting firms are normally submitted in draft form after completion of all field work. These drafts are reviewed and commented on in detail by the Bank staff and the government before the consultant proceeds with printing the final version. Discussion of the draft final report is frequently the occasion of a last supervision mission during which government representatives, consultants, and Bank staff meet in the study area.

Follow-up of study reports normally takes place in the course of (a) project appraisal work, in cases of preinvestment studies that prepare projects for Bank/IDA lending, or (b) normal project supervision, in cases of studies that relate to previous Bank-IDA lending.

Final Observations

The World Bank group includes the International Bank for Reconstruction and Development (IBRD), the International Development Association (IDA), and the International Finance Corporation (IFC). These institutions are dedicated to helping raise standards of living in developing countries by providing financial and technical assistance.

World Bank group policies and procedures are probably the best developed and have been shown effective. The major regional development banks, such as the Inter-American Development Bank, the African Development Bank, and the Asian Development Bank, have similar policies and procedures of their own. None are exactly alike. However, the international financial agencies and development institutions often consult one another and are frequently in touch with consultant matters. Hence, the above-detailed World Bank procedures, which were discussed during a seminar on consulting services at the IBRD a couple of years ago, can be used as general guidelines for almost all internationally financed work. Nevertheless, as new experiences are being gathered, and careful reviews of major worldwide projects take place, changes are bound to occur and policies will be modified from time to time. Therefore, consultants interested in obtaining and executing work for the international development institutions and financing agencies are well advised to maintain continued personal contact with the consultant's liaison officers, project engineers, area desk officers, etc., in order to have a complete understanding of the financier's position and requirements prior to and after entering into any commitments. Usually, the banks and agencies are readily available to meet with consultants and to provide guidance and offer suggestions. It must be understood, however, that there is a limit to what the lending agencies can do for international consultants. In January 1975, the World Bank's file on consultants contained information on nearly 5,000 firms from ninety-five countries who had expressed an interest in being engaged to provide professional services at one time or another.

AGENCY FOR INTERNATIONAL DEVELOPMENT AND EXPORT-IMPORT BANK OF THE UNITED STATES

U.S. consultants have, of course, a particular interest in the State Department's Agency for International Development (AID) and the Export-Import Bank of the United States (Exim). AID, during the past few years, has increasingly concentrated its resources on a limited group of human problems common to many less-developed countries. These include agriculture and food production, with emphasis on human nutrition; population control; health care; and low-cost education. Research and pilot programs designed to yield better solutions to the development problems are still receiving priority. AID, also, has largely shifted its program of grants to U.S. universities and nonprofit organizations, thus losing much of its appeal to independent consultants in private practice. Deeply involved in political developments in Washington and subject to never-ending new controls, limitations, thrusts, and charges, AID periodically issues policy statements and declarations of its activities and accomplishments. These can be obtained directly from Washington by all interested parties.

Playing strictly the role of financier and promoter of exports, the Export-Import Bank rarely, if ever, employs independent consultants. However, projects financed by Export-Import Bank loans through direct credits, Commercial Bank Guarantees, Foreign Credit Insurance, the Cooperating Financing Facility, and discount loans can be executed only by U.S. firms, and, therefore, Exim generates interest and commands the attention of the U.S. consulting community. During the fiscal year ending June 1975, Exim supported $12.5 billion in exports of goods and services. Interest rates are set by weighing two factors: (1) its own cost of money and (2) its congressional mandate to support U.S. exports on competitive terms and conditions. Information concerning Exim activities is available from the Bank at all times, and inquiries and visitors are welcome.

CONCLUSION

In conclusion, consultants providing professional services must recognize the importance of the international institutions and agencies. Governments and local agencies to a very large extent provide the work and select the consultants. The financial institutions, however, supply the funds and, as bankers, dictate many of the terms and conditions under which the projects are to be approached and developed. Consultants who have been successful in negotiating agreements with clients that are internationally financed can expect to have contracts reviewed and conditions and fees questioned by the lenders. A thorough knowledge of applicable policies and procedures contributes to prompt, satisfactory approvals, which in turn benefit all concerned as the project start-up period is thereby accelerated.

The relationships between the lenders and the borrowers are normally quite good. Only a very few borrowers have been known to defy the lender's rules and regulations. Still, differences in interpretation and ever-changing conditions frequently bring about the need for a reassessment of an internationally financed project. Consultants should be in the lead when it comes to project discussions between borrowers and lenders. Therefore a full understanding of the role of both parties and, particularly, the inner workings of the lending agency is of the greatest importance for the successful execution of an internationally financed engagement.

For the convenience of readers, the following pages contain the official names and current addresses of the major international development institutions and financing agencies.

INTERNATIONAL DEVELOPMENT INSTITUTIONS AND FINANCING AGENCIES

African Development Bank
(AFDB)
Boîte Postale 1387
Abidjan
Ivory Coast

Arab Fund for Economic and Social
Development (AF)
P.O. Box 21923
Kuwait

Asian Development Bank (ASDB)
P.O. Box 789
Manila
Philippines

Caribbean Development Bank
(CDB)
P.O. Box 408
Wildey, St. Michael
Barbados, W.I.

Central American Bank
Apartado 772
Tegucigalpa
Honduras

Confederación Latinoamericana de
Cooperativas
de Ahorro y Credito R. L. (COLAC)
Apartado 6664
Panama 5,
Republic of Panama

Department of State
Agency for International
Development (AID)
Washington, D.C. 20523
U.S.A.

Export-Import Bank of the United
States (EXIM)
811 Vermont Avenue
Washington, D.C. 20571
U.S.A.

Food and Agriculture Organization
(FAO)
Via Delle Terme di Caracalla
00100 Rome
Italy

Inter-American Development Bank
(IDB)
808 17th Street, N.W.
Washington, D.C. 20571
U.S.A.

Inter-Governmental Maritime
Consultive Organization (IMCO)
101-104 Picadilly
London VIV OAE
United Kingdom

International Atomic Energy
Agency (IAEA)
Kaertnerring II
A 1010 Vienna 1
Austria

International Bank for
Reconstruction and Development
(IBRD)
1818 H Street, N.W.
Washington, D.C. 20433
U.S.A.

International Civil Aviation
Organization (ICAO)
International Aviation Building
1080 University Street
Montreal 101
Canada

International Development
Association (IDA)
1818 H Street, N.W.
Washington, D.C. 20433
U.S.A.

International Finance Corporation
(IFC)
1818 H Street, N.W.
Washington, D.C. 20433
U.S.A.

International Labour Organisation
(ILO)
Ch1211 Geneva 22
Switzerland

International Monetary Fund
(IMF)
19th and H Streets, N.W.
Washington, D.C. 20006
U.S.A.

International Telecommunication
Union (ITU)
Place Des Nations
1211 Geneva 20
Switzerland

Kuwait Fund for Arab Economic
Development (KF)
P.O. Box 2921
Kuwait

United Nations (UN)
New York, New York 10017
U.S.A.

United Nations Conference on
Trade and Development
(UNCTAD)
Palais Des Nations
1211 Geneva 27
Switzerland

United Nations Development
Programme (UNDP)
New York, New York 10017
U.S.A.

United Nations Educational,
Scientific and Cultural Organization
(UNESCO)
Place De Fontenoy
Paris Ville
France

United Nations Industrial
Development Organization
(UNIDO)
Lerchenfelderstrasse 1, P.O. Box
707
A-1070 Vienna
Austria

Universal Postal Union (UPU)
Weltpoststrasse 4
3000 Bern
Switzerland

World Health Organization (WHO)
Avenue Appia
1211 Geneva 27
Switzerland

World Meteorological Organization
(WMO)
41 Avenue Guiseppe Motta
1211 Geneva 20
Switzerland

TERMINATION OF CONTRACTS, DISPUTES, FORCE MAJEURE, AND INTERNATIONAL ARBITRATION

The performance of consulting services overseas as such is not substantially different from the execution of professional work domestically. However, extraordinary situations that may develop half-way around the globe, while they cannot be foreseen, should nevertheless be manageable for both the international consultant and his foreign client. Of particular concern are natural disasters that periodically befall peoples in distant countries, economic recessions, and political instability. It is important that contractual stipulations provide a basis for harmonious understanding and fair and equitable proceedings, should it become necessary to embark on a course of action that was not originally contemplated.

Let us examine a number of these "special" conditions that ought to be included in international consulting agreements.

TERMINATION OF CONTRACTS

A termination clause in a professional services contract reserves to the client the right to terminate the consultant's work upon due notice for convenience, default, or for force majeure. It defines the obligations of the consultant upon receipt of such notice, as well as the consultant's right to compensation in the event of each type of termination. For example, in the case of termination for convenience, the clause should provide for compensation to the consultant for all expenses incurred in good faith, for the performance of the contract, and for a reasonable fee plus all termination expenses. In case of default by the consultant, the client should not be responsible for payments beyond the accepted and approved performance of the consultant. Should the default be the client's for nonpayment to the consultant, then the client should assume all termination costs and indemnify the consultants to the extent of their specific agreement. Finally, in the case of force majeure, termination of contracts usually is governed by an agreement that the client accepts billings from the consultants for all reasonable expenses to the time of notification plus termination costs, but not for unearned fees.

It may be well to summarize the above by emphasizing that a client can terminate a working relationship with a consultant with or without cause, but that a consultant can terminate normally only for nonpayment, unless additional clauses are provided that specifically spell out what other defaults by the client could lead to the consultant's serving notice of termination.

DISPUTES

Disputes occur more often than not in areas of professional judgment. In the international climate, there exist the additional factors of varied human temperaments, involuntary misunderstandings, widely different education, poor communications, erroneous interpretations, and language variations. Dispute clauses should establish the procedure to be followed with respect to a dispute arising under the terms of a contract.

Settlement of disputes to the satisfaction of the parties can frequently be reached in due course. However, if a first effort of conciliation fails, it may be beneficial to have a second opportunity to reconcile the difference(s). For that purpose, dispute clauses should also establish the manner and method of appealing from any decision on such a dispute.

FORCE MAJEURE

The *American Heritage Dictionary of the English Language* describes force majeure as "an unexpected or uncontrolled event that upsets one's plans or releases one from obligations." Consulting contract language needs to be more specific. Agreement must be reached with a client in advance as to what constitutes force majeure in his particular country. A 10-inch rainfall within twenty-four hours in Western Europe may well be regarded as a major disaster leading to force majeure conditions. In the rain forests of Brazil's northeast or in Liberia, such an event is a common occurrence during the rainy season.

Essentially, force majeure clauses are necessary to determine acts beyond the control of the client and the consultant. They establish the conditions that would excuse a consultant, temporarily or permanently, from performing all or part of his obligations; likewise, they similarly apply to the client under the same conditions. Force majeure clauses prescribe the procedures that should be followed by both the client and the consultant with respect to notification and determination of any such condition. Also, they set forth the consultant's and the client's rights and obligations with regard to temporary suspension of work, payment of compensation and expenses, evacuation of personnel, and transport of instruments and equipment. Finally, force majeure clauses provide the appropriate steps that have to be taken in case of contract termination.

INTERNATIONAL ARBITRATION

Because of worldwide interest in international arbitration, the Conference on Security and Cooperation in Europe, popularly called the "Helsinki Conference of 1975," adopted a resolution on private commercial arbitration as it relates to world trade. As a matter of interest, the following is the official English-language text taken from a volume published by the U.S. Department of State:

> The High Representatives of the participating States have solemnly adopted the following: The participating States, considering that the prompt and equitable settlement of disputes which may arise from commercial transactions relating to goods and services and contracts for industrial cooperation would contribute to expanding and facilitating trade and cooperation, considering that arbitration is an appropriate means of settling such disputes, recommend, where appropriate, to organizations, enterprises and firms in their countries, to include arbitration clauses in commercial contracts and industrial cooperation contracts, or in special agreements; recommend that the provision on arbitration should provide for arbitration under a mutually acceptable set of arbitration rules, and permit arbitration in a third country, taking into account existing intergovernmental and other agreements in this field.

Arbitration has not always been accepted and is still rejected by a number of sovereign governments in the lesser-developed countries. The above resolution is of particular significance, therefore, as arbitration is of undisputed value to individuals and firms providing consulting services in foreign countries.

The administration of justice with its manifold ramifications is slow and costly practically everywhere around the world: Courts of law generally carry heavy case loads, and legal proceedings involve substantial expenses. Practices and procedures in some nations make it extremely difficult to pursue perfectly legitimate grievances before politically appointed judges. Time-consuming reviews and obligatory appeals may have to follow original judgments.

Arbitration, therefore, is a most acceptable means for the settlement of disputes. International consultants should include a provision in their service contracts for arbitration of disputes by an impartial body, wherever possible. When the law of a local country does not recognize arbitration or prohibits the intervention of internationally recognized authorities, alternative arrangements should be sought.

International bodies offering arbitration services frequently mentioned in consulting agreements are:

The Court of Arbitration
International Chamber of Commerce
38 Cours Albert 1er
Paris, France 75008

The American Arbitration Association
140 West 51st Street
New York, N.Y. 10020
U.S.A.

Both the Court of Arbitration of the International Chamber of Commerce and the American Arbitration Association can provide the services of individual arbitrators. More important, however, is the fact that they have established procedures, rules, and regulations that will guide arbitration proceedings.

Another institution offering arbitration services is the International Centre for Settlement of Investment Disputes. Established in 1965 by the Convention on the Settlement of Investment Disputes between States and Nationals of Other States, the Centre functions as an autonomous member of the prestigious World Bank group in Washington, D.C. The purpose of the Centre is to be available to the parties to international investment arrangements in providing them with an assured forum on which they may agree for the settlement of any future disputes. They will also assist them, through conciliation or arbitration procedures, in settling any disputes that have already arisen.

As a number of sovereign nations do not accept arbitration clauses in official contracts and will not honor arbitration awards outside of their constitutional court system, the advent of the World Bank's International Centre for Settlement of Investment Disputes offering conciliation and arbitration facilities is of considerable interest to the international consulting sector. Since a large percentage of all consulting work overseas is connected with or related to investment activities, consultants clearly can benefit from the ICSID.

The 15 November 1975 bulletin of the International Centre for Settlement of Investment Disputes lists the following contracting states that officially recognize and are disposed toward acceptance of ICSID conciliation and arbitration services:

Afghanistan
Austria
Belgium
Botswana
Burundi
Cameroon
Central African Republic
Chad
Republic of China
People's Republic of the Congo
Cyprus
Dahomey
Denmark
Egypt
Finland
France
Gabon
West Germany (including Berlin)
Ghana
Greece
Guinea
Guyana
Iceland
Indonesia
Italy
Ivory Coast
Jamaica
Japan
Jordan
Kenya
South Korea
Lesotho
Liberia
Luxembourg
Malagasy Republic
Malawi
Malaysia
Mauritania
Mauritius
Morocco
Nepal
Netherlands
Niger
Nigeria
Norway
Pakistan
Senegal
Sierra Leone
Somalia
Sri Lanka
Sudan
Swaziland
Sweden
Switzerland
Togo
Trinidad and Tobago
Tunisia
Uganda
United Kingdom of Great Britain and Northern Ireland
United States of America
Upper Volta
Yugoslavia
Zaire
Zambia

Latin America as a whole and many Mid-East countries do not permit arbitration clauses in their contracts. Thus, to avoid compulsory court action in case of disputes that cannot be settled among the parties, consultants may be well advised to confer with host-country attorneys in an effort to develop means and ways that can provide a satisfactory solution for out-of-court proceedings that are meaningful and effective.

Arbitration clauses vary from country to country and from case to case. The international financial institutions and development agencies have developed language that can often serve as a guideline for agreements in the public and private sectors.

It is often said that contracts are only as good as the goodwill of the contracting parties. No doubt this is true. But honest differences of opinion and judgment do occur from time to time in the performance of international engagements. Thus the provision of protective clauses for speedy and satisfactory settlements of disagreements is an important consideration to the international consultant in negotiating and executing contracts.

PROFESSIONAL LIABILITY, INSURANCE, AND BONDS AND GUARANTEES

PROFESSIONAL LIABILITY

Professionals throughout the United States are in the midst of what some authorities term a legal explosion. The private practice of consulting is vulnerable to claims of professional liability.

Charges of professional negligence are a very serious matter. Even if the final outcome of proceedings proves that charges are without merit and vindicates the consultant, consequential damage to the professional's reputation can be lasting and beyond repair. The cost of defense against liability suits can easily exceed the total of fees earned for any given engagement.

It should be understood that litigation of any type is an outcome of controversy. Professional liability claims are therefore the result of disputes in professional areas of expertise and are frequently caused by a failure of communications and a deterioration in relations between the consultant and client. Minor clashes have a tendency to be cumulative. If permitted to continue and to build up, there follows the threat of a total breakdown leading to litigation, termination, and penalties.

Generally, claims against professional liability are as complicated to prove as they are difficult to counter.

In the international marketplace, a consultant's responsibility is not different from that within the United States. As yet, however, legal proceedings overseas against professionals are relatively rare. A serious dispute between a foreign consultant and his overseas client can bring about the consultant's blacklisting for any further engagements in that country. The international financing institutions and development agencies maintain performance records on all consultants performing professional services that are institutionally supported. Thus, charges of professional negligence, omissions and errors, and poor judgment leveled against a consulting firm in a Latin American country may have repercussions halfway around the world in South Asia.

Whereas U.S. liability suits lead increasingly to courts of law and occasional out-of-court settlements, foreign disputes involving consulting practices and professional judgment generally oblige international consultants to voluntarily institute remedial action. This involves time-consuming and costly reviews and may necessitate the provision of services for which it will not be possible to collect reasonable compensation.

Clearly, the most important step to avoid liability controversy is to assure that communications on all levels are well established, perfectly understood, and painstakingly maintained from the very beginning of a consultant-to-client relationship to the final receipt of a letter of acceptance or the official completion of an assignment. Likewise, no effort should be spared to approach overseas assignments with an understanding of human relations and basic psychology.

Professional liability insurance policies are available to most established consultants. Premiums are substantial and increase as claims accumulate. Deductibles vary but tend to be high. So far, insurance companies throughout the world differentiate little between domestic and foreign risks so long as the insured has demonstrated the capability to perform credibly. Strictly domestic policies, however, should be endorsed to cover international engagements. Riders can be secured for specific work abroad; worldwide coverage is available to established individuals and firms from a number of insurers in many countries. The governments of Germany, France, Great Britain, and Japan underwrite special risks for their nationals, particularly when services are provided to an official host-government agency.

Associations, joint ventures, and partnerships with foreign individuals and firms are not normally included in standard professional liability insurance policies. Care must be taken to apply for adequate protection.

Insurance coverage for professional liability in foreign lands is frequently written into a domestic policy in the form of an endorsement. Sometimes, separate policies are issued for large overseas engagements. In either case, consultants should instruct their insurance agents to provide coverage for especially pertinent hazards of an international practice, such as the high costs of communications and travel, mobilization and demobilization, legal expenses of domestic and foreign attorneys, and translations.

Occasionally, claims of professional liability may motivate a local client to confiscate his foreign consultant's physical assets and to freeze his funds. As the final disposition of a complicated overseas case may take a long time, there too a consultant may benefit from appropriate insurance coverage.

American insurance companies are not always able or willing to write policies to the full satisfaction of a consultant. Lloyd's of London and other international insurance brokers serve the needs of many individuals and firms throughout the world. As long as professional liability constitutes an element of risk, consultants are well advised to protect themselves with the most comprehensive insurance coverage that can be obtained at a reasonable premium.

INSURANCE

The preceding chapters of this book have repeatedly contained references to insurance. This paragraph itemizes areas of special foreign risks and exposure for which international consultants may wish to consider full or partial overseas coverage.

- Comprehensive general liability
- Legal liability
- Professional liability
- Employee liability
- Commercial credit risks:
  - Client's failure to pay
  - Client's insolvency
- Political risks:
  - Failure to transfer local funds into foreign exchange
  - Cancellation of licenses or permits
  - War, hostilities, civil war, rebellion, revolution, insurrection, civil commotion
  - Requisition, expropriation, confiscation intervention
- Joint ventures, associations
- Medical, hospitalization, life
- Accident, personal injury
- Travel accident
- Property, housing, offices, and personal belongings
  - Fire, lightning, explosions

- Vandalism
- Earthquakes, floods
- Political risks

Investments

- Commercial risks
- Political risks

Kidnapping, extortion

Inflation risk

Comprehensive general liability covers all liability arising out of declared occupational hazards, including the cost of defense. For overseas engagements, it is recommended that false arrest, libel, slander, and defamation of character be added.

Legal liability should be validated for the employment of foreign counsel in addition to normal domestic legal assistance.

Professional liability has already been discussed in detail above.

Employee liability is partially contained in domestic (U.S.) workmen's compensation but should be extended for international protection. This may be accomplished through the consultant's established carrier, or through mandatory or voluntary host-country institutions.

Commercial credit risks, as well as *political risks,* are insurable in the United States by the Foreign Credit Insurance Association (FCIA) and the Export-Import Bank. A number of industrialized nations have similar government-sponsored insurance programs—for instance COFACE in France, Hermes Kreditversicherung GmBH in Germany, and ECGD in Great Britain. Commercial and political risk coverage generally requires official backing from host-government agencies. Many, but not all the lesser-developed nations have expressed their readiness to issue government guarantees in return for the availability of this kind of insurance. Consultants should contact their insurance brokers to confirm that commercial and political risks in a particular country are insurable.

Joint ventures and associations need explicit insurance coverage clauses in standard policies, or can be insured separately for specific engagements.

Overseas coverage for *medical, hospitalization, life, accident, and personal injury* is different from domestic insurance only to the extent that foreign billings will be accepted by the insurance carriers to cover illness and accidents occurring overseas.

Travel accident, likewise, should specifically permit foreign travel and provide for higher limits than equivalent domestic insurance policies.

Property, housing, offices, and personal belongings of the consultant and his employees are best given extended coverage by including a number of specified risks not commonly named in domestic insurance documents. It may be interesting to note that flood insurance was extremely hard to obtain in the United States until the government stepped in and established a special program. Overseas, however, flood insurance is quite ordinary and commands a very negligible premium.

Investment insurance is similar to political and commercial risk insurance and handled, if not totally by government agencies, at least in part with official support. U.S. consultants should familiarize themselves with the practices of the Overseas Private Investment Corporation (OPIC) in Washington, D.C.

Terrorism has become unfortunately all too frequent during the past decade. Prominent consultants have been targets of ambitious subversive groups in several countries. Large sums of money are sought in return for the release of an unfortunate victim of ruthless kidnappers. Ransom demands by far exceed the life savings of most professionals; few consulting firms are in the position to meet them.

Kidnap insurance has been in existence for many years in the private sector. It is only the recent wave of extortion and kidnappings that has brought about an acute interest in *kidnapping* insurance by concerned consultants. Obviously, a kidnapping insurance policy is a two-sided protection. Should its existence become known to unscrupulous individuals, a disaster would be invited rather than averted. Consultants will have to decide their course of action in this area according to their particular circumstances. Unhappily, the risk of terrorism cannot be entirely ignored.

Inflation risk insurance was pioneered by France many years ago and is taking on increasing importance. Already COFACE's efforts are being matched by Britain's ECGD and the Japanese. *Inflation risk* insurance is furnished almost exclusively by governments through quasi-official agencies. The U.S. government so far has refused to support inflation risk insurance, arguing that it is illegal in international trade. Concerned consultants entering into several years' practice in inflation-prone nations should investigate the availability of this desirable coverage.

The field of insurance in general is complicated and highly specialized. Insurance brokers are generally respected businessmen and should be consulted in matters relating to international activities and prevailing risks with which a professional might not be fully acquainted.

Insurance premiums are charged to overhead accounts and qualify occasionally as direct reimbursable project costs.

BONDS AND GUARANTEES

Design-constructors and general contractors have traditionally been accustomed to furnishing bonds to guarantee bids, performance, payment advances, materials, general workmanship, and equipment covering the development of physical facilities.

Consultants rendering intellectual services have not been required to place bonds or provide guarantees. Professionals do not present bids but propose to provide services and then negotiate detailed contracts. They stake their reputation on the achievement of excellence. While professional consultants specify materials and equipment, they do not assume responsibility for its manufacture and installation.

Occasionally consultants are required by clients to provide a bank guarantee or a bond in return for the receipt of advance payments or the establishment of revolving funds. This is not an unreasonable demand and can be met without major difficulties. Banks abroad underwrite guarantees for a small consideration, and insurance companies in many parts of the world issue surety bonds at reasonable premiums.

During the past few years, international consultants performing professional services abroad have come under pressure from powerful clients in the Third World to bid for contracts and to secure these with bank guarantees or surety bonds.

Controversy over the quality of intellectual performance is extremely difficult to resolve as it requires professional and independent judgment. Who in the emerging nations has the experience, qualification, and independence to determine if a foreign consultant has indeed failed in the execution of his contractual duties to the extent that his performance bond should be cashed?

Furthermore, demands for bank performance guarantees draw directly on a professional's line of credit, limiting his working capital and increasing greatly the financial risks of such an undertaking. Reports circulated recently speak of guarantees of 5 to 10 percent on bid bonds; 5 to 15 percent of the total project cost (not 5 to 15 percent of the consultant's fee) for performance, and, at times, an additional 10 percent for retention certificates, payable from 10 to 15 years after the completion of the work.

Despite the inherent possible pitfalls of bidding for service contracts and providing bonds, the lure of lucrative work has tempted some international consultants to accept professional engagements on non-professional terms. A number of governments from the industrialized nations, notably the Japanese, actually encourage their nationals "to bid on bonded contracts" by underwriting guarantees on a government-to-government basis.

Bonds and guarantees are generally available to the international consulting industry. Our national bank system is prevented from extending credit guarantees under current legislative restriction; instead, surety bonds are commonly furnished within the United States and for international engagements where these are acceptable. Banks in Europe, Hong Kong, Singapore, Japan, Panama, the Bahamas, and elsewhere "sell" credit guarantees as a commercial service. Letters of credit are accepted everywhere in lieu of bonds and guarantees. These, of course, can be opened through any prime American bank.

Personally I have not been inclined to bid for professional services or to provide performance bonds and guarantees other than to cover payment advances and revolving funds. Ultimately, of course, it is the professional consultant's prerogative to decide if he or she wishes to get involved in bond and guarantee matters or not.

INDEX